Debt as Po

MANCHESTER
1824

Manchester University Press

THEORY FOR A GLOBAL AGE

Series Editor: Gurminder K. Bhambra

Globalization is widely viewed as a current condition of the world, but there is little engagement with how this changes the way we understand it. The *Theory for a Global Age* series addresses the impact of globalization on the social sciences and humanities. Each title will focus on a particular theoretical issue or topic of empirical controversy and debate, addressing theory in a more global and interconnected manner. With contributions from scholars across the globe, the series will explore different perspectives to examine globalization from a global viewpoint. True to its global character, the *Theory for a Global Age* series will be available for online access worldwide via Creative Commons licensing, aiming to stimulate wide debate within academia and beyond.

Previously published by Bloomsbury:
Connected Sociologies
Gurminder K. Bhambra

*Eurafrica: The Untold History of
European Integration and Colonialism*
Peo Hansen and Stefan Jonsson

*On Sovereignty and Other
Political Delusions*
Joan Cocks

*Postcolonial Piracy: Media Distribution and
Cultural Production in the Global South*
Edited by Lars Eckstein and Anja Schwarz

*The Black Pacific: Anti-Colonial
Struggles and Oceanic Connections*
Robbie Shilliam

Democracy and Revolutionary Politics
Neera Chandhoke

**Published by Manchester
University Press:**
*John Dewey: The Global Public
and Its Problems*
John Narayan

Debt as Power

Tim Di Muzio and Richard H. Robbins

Manchester University Press

Published by Manchester University Press
Altrincham Street, Manchester M1 7JA

www.manchesteruniversitypress.co.uk

British Library Cataloguing-in-Publication Data
A catalogue record for this book is available from the British Library

Library of Congress Cataloging-in-Publication Data applied for

ISBN   978 1 7849 93252   hardback
        978 1 7849 93269   paperback
        978 1 5261 01013   open access

First published 2016

Typeset by
Integra Software Services Pvt. Ltd.
Printed in Great Britain by
Bell and Bain Ltd, Glasgow

For Verónica

The Debt

By Paul Laurence Dunbar (1872–1906)

This is the debt I pay
Just for one riotous day,
Years of regret and grief,
Sorrow without relief.

Pay it I will to the end –
Until the grave, my friend,
Gives me a true release –
Gives me the clasp of peace.

Slight was the thing I bought,
Small was the debt I thought,
Poor was the loan at best –
God! but the interest!

Contents

Series Editor's Foreword

"Debt" is a seemingly universal and constant aspect of human experience and history. However, the social practices and economic structures that are involved need to be understood through the global interconnections that give form to its historical instantiations as well as its contemporary manifestations. This is the compelling claim of Tim Di Muzio and Richard H. Robbin's book *Debt as Power* and, as such, fits perfectly into the Theory for a Global Age series that seeks to take "global interconnections" as the basis from which to rethink both conceptual frameworks and commonly held understandings.

In *Debt as Power*, Di Muzio and Robbins present a historical account of the modern origins of capitalist debt by looking at how commercial money is produced as debt in the late seventeenth and early eighteenth centuries. They expertly demonstrate their key contention—that debt is a technology of power—and identify the ways in which the control, production, and distribution of money, as interest-bearing debt, are used to discipline populations. Their sharp analysis brings together histories of the development of the Bank of England and the establishment of permanent national debt with the intensification and expansion of debt, as a "technology of power", under colonialism in a global context. The latter part of the book addresses the consequences of modern regimes of debt and puts forward proposals of what needs to be done, politically, to reverse the problems generated by debt-based economies. The final chapter presents a convincing case for the 99% to use the power of debt to challenge present inequalities and outlines a platform for action suggesting possible alternatives.

This ambitious book is both a diagnosis of our current social and economic global condition structured by the debt–credit nexus and a clarion call to action. Action is necessary if we are to overturn the manifold miseries associated with debt and bring about a more equal distribution, not only of wealth, but also of societal well-being. It is possible, as Di Muzio and Robbins forcefully argue, that the very survival of humanity depends on it.

Gurminder K. Bhambra

1

Toward a Stark Utopia

*Our thesis is that the idea of a self-adjusting market implied a
stark utopia. Such an institution could not exist for any length of
time without annihilating the human and natural substance of
society; it would have physically destroyed man and transformed
his surroundings into a wilderness. Inevitably, society took
measures to protect itself, but whatever measures it took impaired
the self-regulation of the market, disorganized industrial life, and
thus endangered society in yet another way. It was this dilemma
which forced the development of the market system into a definite
groove and finally disrupted the social organization based upon it.
(Polanyi 1944: 3–4)*

On November 20, 2003, in the rural countryside of India, Nagalinga
Reddy, a farmer of rice and sunflowers, committed suicide. At fifty
years of age, Reddy took his life by ingesting ammonium phosphate
tablets—a pesticide used in modernized farming. His rice crops
had just failed due to pests and he was deeply in debt to usurious
moneylenders, three banks, and a cooperative. He was harassed
regularly by his creditors, and he finally put an end to their tyranny
by taking his life.[1] But Reddy's suicide was no isolated incident. Since
1995, there has been what can only be described as an epidemic
of farmer suicides in India. *The Hindu* reports that from 1995 to
2010, 256,913 farmers have taken their lives—the vast majority by
ingesting the very same pesticide swallowed by Reddy.[2] According to
the Center for Human Rights and Global Justice and P. Sainath, who
has covered the epidemic in India, the common link between these

suicides is punishing personal indebtedness to local moneylenders and/or microfinance institutions (2011: 1; Deshpande and Arora 2010; Young 2010; Taylor 2012). But the epidemic has another contributing factor: the neoliberal reforms introduced in India in 1991. To regain the confidence of creditors in its burgeoning budget and trade deficit as well as mounting national debt, the Indian government accepted neoliberal reforms in exchange for a loan from the International Monetary Fund (IMF) (Chossudovsky 2002: 149ff; McCartney in Saad-Filho and Johnston 2005: 238).[3] To ensure debt service to rich creditors, economic reforms hit many agricultural communities particularly hard. Many farmers experienced mounting costs for energy and basic inputs like fertilizer. These goods were once subsidized by the government, but with the turn to neoliberal austerity in the 1990s, farming was increasingly financed through the personal debt of farmers and their families. This politico-agricultural transformation has led to land dispossession, the concentration of land in fewer hands, and widespread farmer suicides (Mohanty 2005; Levien 2011; 2012; 2013).

In the rural countryside of Thailand, we find another story of humanity in the global age. Nok is a woman raised in rural Thailand and a seemingly willful participant in her own trafficking to Japan. According to her own account, her father was deeply in debt to credit and agricultural cooperatives because the money the family made from rice farming was insufficient to repay the interest, let alone the principal. In this predicament, Nok's older sister had agreed to be trafficked to Japan in return for paying a debt of 3.5 million yen (about $34,000) to her traffickers. She worked in the sex industry and eventually paid down her debt, enabling her to send more money back home. Nok soon followed in her sister's footsteps and used the same trafficker to become a sex worker in Japan (Aoyama 2009: 85ff). Like the farmer suicides of India, this is no isolated incident. Countless Thai women have been trafficked not only to Japan and surrounding region but also to brothels in their home country. The practice typically begins when a family is encouraged to sell their daughter to a broker who promises to get them cash work in the city. The transaction is too often made so that the family can use the money to overcome economic hardship (e.g., to repay mortgages on rice fields) and even acquire some of the trappings of modernity (e.g., television and electrical appliances).[4] This begins what can only be called a debt trap:

> The contractual arrangement between the broker and parents requires that this money be repaid by the daughter's labor before she is free to leave or is allowed to send money home. Sometimes the money is treated as a loan to the parents, the girl being both the collateral and the means of repayment. In such cases the exorbitant interest charged on the loan means there is little chance that a girl's sexual slavery will ever repay the debt. (Bales 2012: 41).

As Jefferies notes, this practice is not isolated to Thailand: "trafficking in women and girls into debt bondage is becoming the main method of supply for national and international sex industries. It is worth $31 billion yearly according to UN estimates" (2009: 152).

The dismal epidemic of farmer suicides and sex trafficking have also corresponded with a rise in organ trafficking. Medical research and modern technology have made organ transplants more routine, potentially elongating and improving the lives of a lucky few who have access to donors and capable surgeons. But this medical advance also has a dark side. Poverty, debt, and desperation have helped fuel a growing international trade in human organs. The trade is often illicit but appears to be happening with increasing frequency among vulnerable populations (Scheper-Hughes 2000; Territo and Matteson 2011; Decker 2014). In rural Bangladesh, what Moniruzzaman (2012) calls a "body bazzar" has emerged to take advantage of mounting debt levels due to the microcredit revolution and the financialization of the countryside. Microcredit is the extension of small non-collateral-backed loans. The loans are made with the belief that the poor will use this money to become entrepreneurial and eventually better their economic and social conditions. While this revolution has been celebrated by many for lifting poor women and men out of poverty, it has also been heavily criticized for capitalizing the most vulnerable and creating mini-debt traps that can spiral out of control. For example, with the introduction of credit into rural Bangladesh, many Bangladeshis who have taken loans are finding it difficult to repay their creditors. Some, such as Mohammad Akhta Alam, were in debt to more than one nongovernmental organization specializing in microcredit. The more wealthy and educated take advantage of desperate debtors, who are mostly illiterate and uneducated, and convince them to sell one of their kidneys, liver lobes, or corneas. When Alam could not repay his debt, an organ broker persuaded him to sell one of his kidneys. In desperation, Alam accepted the offer and is now partially paralyzed and blind in one eye. He can no longer do any heavy lifting. What makes matters worse is the money Alam was promised was never paid in full—he received only a fraction of the total promised to him. In his own words, Alam says, "I agreed to sell my kidney because I couldn't return the money to the NGOs. As we are poor and helpless, that is why we are bound to do this. I regret it."[5] Alam's experience is not unique. As Moniruzzaman's (2012) ethnography reveals, this type of "bio-violence" is increasingly common in Bangladesh. Although it is not always the case that people commodify their bodily organs for money to service their debts (some just do it for the extra money), debt has been a primary driver of the trade as identified in at least Brazil, Malaysia, Pakistan, India, Iran, Iraq, Indonesia, Israel, Egypt, Serbia, Philippines, Vietnam, Mexico, South Africa, the United States, and China.

In a world of increasing commodification, education itself has become a commodity increasingly capitalized by investors. Nowhere is this more true than in the United States, where students now collectively owe $1.2 trillion to the US government and myriad banks and private lenders. The average student debt is $30,000, with some students finishing their education with debt as large as $150,000. Some will be able to service their debts and eventually repay them when they find decent employment. Many others, however, will have difficulty finding jobs with decent pay and hence struggle to service their interest-bearing loans throughout their lives. With few exceptions, student loans can never be discharged through bankruptcy and many may go to their graves still in hock for pursuing an education. In fact, crushing debt burdens have already influenced some to take their own lives and many more have daily thoughts of suicide.[6] Others suffer from acute stress, anxiety, and depression. For its part, the US government is doing precious little, largely because of bipartisan bickering and the influence of the banking lobby on Congress. With 40 million students leaving college with debt, the United States is looking more and more like a debtocracy than a democracy.[7]

The Global Financial Crisis of 2007–8 was in reality a global debt crisis. Many nations are still affected, but the case of Greece is particularly stark for its social dislocations and violence. Kouvelakis (2011) has argued that the debt crisis in Greece must be understood within the historical trajectory of Greece's development that emerged after the dictatorship (1967–74). From 1981, successive administrations built up a social welfare state with a large public sector and generous entitlements such as jobs for life and generous pensions. The government also bought considerable military hardware from abroad and financed the 2004 Olympics construction. To pay for these projects, government elites borrowed from foreign creditors while many wealthy citizens underreported their income for tax purposes or evaded taxes altogether. From 1981 to 2007, the national debt ballooned from roughly 27 percent of gross domestic product (GDP) to 105 percent by the time of the crisis. In 2014 that figure stands at 153 percent of GDP. Eventually, this debt became unsustainable and forced Greece into the hands of the EU–ECB–IMF, commonly known as the troika. The overall assessment was that the population was living beyond its means, and in order to receive new loans to service the old ones, the government would have to enact severe cuts to its social spending. Public sector salaries and pensions were slashed and public assets sold off to raise funds to repay creditors—a pattern, as we shall see, that has been recurrent in previous national debt crises. Not surprisingly, political upheaval and social unrest soon followed as the population turned its anger toward elite corruption, kleptocracy, and foreigners. Multiple reasons have been given for the debt crisis, from corruption and tax evasion to a bloated public sector (Manolopoulos 2011). But one thing is certain: debt has led to a generalized politics of austerity with the most vulnerable suffering the most, as the Greek tragedy continues to unfold.

• • •

What unites these seemingly discrete moments of crisis and hardship that cut across both geographical space and historical time? Despite circumstantial differences, they are all social acts or practices that can be traced to the prevalence of debt. The world is awash in debt, and though we should recognize that debt levels and access to credit are radically unequal within and between countries, the commonality of all modern political economies is not so much that they are market oriented but that *they are all debt-based political economies*. Indeed, as Rowbotham noted, "the world can be considered a single debt-based economy" (1998: 159). To take an international perspective, according to the global management consulting firm McKinsey and Co., as of the second quarter of 2014 the total outstanding debt across 183 countries was $199 trillion.[8] In 1990, the same figure was only $45 trillion or a 342 percent increase over the period (McKinsey 2013). As identified in Table 1.1, since 2000 all categories of debt have increased considerably with government debt, financial industry debt, and household debt leading the categories.

Table 1.1 Total global debt by category

Type of debt	2000 (4Q) Dollar (trillion)	2007 (4Q) Dollar (trillion)	2014 (2Q) Dollar (trillion)	Percent increase (%) since 2000
Government bonds	22	33	58	163
Financial bonds	20	37	45	125
Corporate bonds	26	38	56	46
Household	20	33	40	100
Total debt as a % of GDP	246	269	286	16

Source: McKinsey (2015: 15).

But the concept and prevalence of debt in capitalist modernity needs to be critically theorized. Our starting point, and primary argument, is that debt within capitalist modernity is a social technology of power and its continued deployment heralds a stark utopia. Our claim is not that debt *can be thought of* as a technology of power but rather that debt *is* a technology of power. By technology, we simply mean a skill, art, or manner of doing something connected to a form of rationality or logic and mobilized by definite social forces. In capitalism, the prevailing logic is the logic of differential accumulation, and given that *debt instruments far outweigh equity instruments*, we can safely claim that interest-bearing debt is the primary way in which economic inequality is generated as more money is redistributed to creditors. In other words, debt instruments effectively divide society into debtors and creditors within a power structure that vastly privileges the latter over the former. However, we know this is a bold claim to make, but we hope by the end of this book, the reader will be convinced of our argument and inspired to learn more and take political action.

A brief review of debt scholarship

The literature on debt cuts across the social sciences and is relatively vast. For this reason we cannot hope to offer a comprehensive review of the literature. However, as it currently stands, the literature can be divided into major groupings that address different, albeit, interrelated concerns: (1) the origin of the national debt (Omond 1870; Denby 1916; Hamilton 1947); (2) debt within and throughout history (Geisst 2013; Graeber 2013; Kwarteng 2014); (3) the debt crises of the 1980s in the Global South (Payer 1974; George 1988; 1992; Griffith-Jones 1989); (4) the current sovereign debt crises of the Global North (Pettifor 2006; Chorafas 2011; Lane 2012; Greer 2014); (5) odious debt (Bonilla 2011; Manolopoulos 2011; Ndikumana and Boyce 2011); and (6) country-specific debt crises and struggles to find alternatives (Rowbotham 1998; Lin 2003; Brown

2007; 2013; Bonner and Wiggin 2009; Dienst 2011; Soederberg 2012; 2013a; 2013b; Jackson and Dyson 2013; Pettifor 2014).

For the most part, these are all valuable contributions to our knowledge. However, our study seeks to cut across these boundaries to provide a more foundational, historically sensitive, and comprehensive theorization of debt as an interconnected global phenomenon. In this light, our book is unique for two main reasons.

First, rather than focus on the historical emergence of debt as a moral obligation, country-specific debt, or periodic financial crises related to debt, we are interested in the production of commercial money as debt under capitalism. We argue that under capitalism, debt is a *technology of power*, intimately connected with the control, creation, and allocation of modern money, the requirement for perpetual growth, and the differential capitalization that benefits what has recently, and aptly, been called "the 1%"—particularly the owners of money-creating instruments (Di Muzio 2014). Thus, what we are interested in is how the control, production, and allocation of money as interest-bearing debt gets capitalized by private social forces and what this means for the majority of people on the planet. This is incredibly important since after oil and gas, banking is the most heavily capitalized sector on the planet, with the largest banks by market capitalization valued at $4.4 trillion dollars (Di Muzio 2012).[9] The owners or investors of these banks capitalize the banking sector's power to create money as interest-bearing debt—the major source of the banking sector's profits. This is highly troublesome but not just for systemic risk and future financial crises, as the IMF has pointed out.[10] When we consider the question of differential power, it is worrisome because of the following:

(1) We know that only a small minority of individuals and families own the majority of shares in publically listed banks and that this ownership is largely hidden from public scrutiny.[11]

(2) We know that the banking sector is highly interconnected with banks owning shares in each other as well as other corporations (Vitali et al. 2011).

(3) The ability to create money as interest-bearing debt out of nothing is an incredible power that funnels money upward to the owners and executives of banks as they collect interest and fees on needed credit.

(4) Given that loans are contingent on creditworthiness and past wealth accumulation, there is *always* a hierarchy of access to money with the already rich having far easier access to credit and thus far more advantages to accumulate wealth.

(5) Democracy is held at ransom by the banks insofar as our elected governments have tacitly agreed to let private individuals and families capitalize the supply of money required for economic interdependence in a market economy. We historicize and elaborate on each of these points in the ensuing chapters.

The second reason this book is unique is that we follow Ingham (2004) and others (see e.g., Piketty 2014: 573ff) in recognizing that the ossified disciplinary boundaries that originated with the *Methodenstreit* are largely unhelpful if we want to understand the social relations of capitalism. For this reason, we approach our study with what we call an "interconnected historical holism." What we mean by this term is a mode of historical inquiry that begins with the recognition that the histories of human communities and their natural environments are interconnected in complex spatial and hierarchical relations of power. We suggest that to understand their development we need to examine not only the particularities of a given human community and their cultural practices but more importantly their interconnected, interdependent, and international dimensions (Bhambra 2007; 2010). Since all modern economies are debt economies, this leads us to a more holistic account of debt as a technology of power within capitalist modernity. Since debt under capitalism is increasingly ubiquitous at all levels of society and economic growth (and austerity) is now virtually the sole mantra of dominant political parties around the world, we argue that tracing some of the major inflections in the evolution and effects of debt as a technology of power is crucial for understanding the "present as history" and for suggesting possible alternatives to our current trajectory. But as Mann reminds us, "ubiquity, however, is not uniformity" (2003: 3). The hierarchy, meaning, and culture of indebtedness is not static, but a fluid continuum within and between political communities.

It is not our intent to do a review of the extensive literature, much of it recent, on debt and its impact. However, two highly publicized works relate directly to our work, one, David Graeber's *Debt: A 5000 Year History*, explicitly addressing debt, and the other, Thomas Piketty's *Capital in the Twenty-First Century*, implicitly addressing it and the distribution and creation of power over social reproduction (Bakker and Gill 2003). Given the magnitude and timeliness of both Graeber's book on debt and Piketty's on capital, it is important to show how our work is distinct from theirs and how they both inform our arguments.

Graeber's starting point seems to be how social obligations eventually turn into pecuniary debts that are quantifiable. From this point he stumbles upon power and argues that debts are typically enforced and facilitated by violence or the threat of punishment and that a market economy is largely the result of war, conquest, and slavery (2013: 385). But Graeber does not sufficiently theorize the power underpinnings of debt in a society governed by markets and the price system—power is not his starting point, but a supporting actor in a much larger 5,000-year historico-anthropology of debt.[12] Unlike Graeber, our starting point is the presence of power as a differential social relation, and we theorize debt not just as money owed but as a technology of differential power over others rooted in private ownership. So whereas Graeber muses that "what makes debt different is that it is premised on an assumption of equality," we argue the exact opposite: the very foundation of modern capitalist debt is premised upon inequality or "differential power"— our preferred term (2011: 86). This point leads us to consider, to our knowledge for the first time in this light, not just the *private* control over the production and allocation of money but its very ownership and capitalization.[13] It is only from this starting point, we reason, that we can begin to think about debt within capitalist modernity in its interconnected and international dimensions. This is the second point of difference our work has with Graeber's erudite and impressive study: we do not offer a sweeping history of debt across millennia but have the far more modest goal of trying to understand the role of debt as a technology of power in the emergence and development of capitalist modernity. Of course, we recognize with Ingham's sympathetic critique of Graeber's work that "a long developmental sequence" was certainly involved in producing current levels and practices of debt (2013: 135). But while retracing millennia of human history may be intellectually stimulating, we reason with Polanyi ([1944] 1957) that capitalism was such a decisive break with previous forms of human economy that it warrants closer scrutiny than Graeber's study permitted.[14] A third point of departure from Graeber's work is that in historicizing the emergence of capitalism we postulate an energy–debt–money nexus, whereby the expansion of the money supply through the creation of interest-bearing loans is *assisted* (not determined) by the surplus energy of fossil fuels (oil, coal, and natural gas).[15] In other words, *countries that have high levels of total final energy consumption will also be economies with large money supplies and mounting levels of debt*. We find this empirically verifiable, and as such, our observations have important implications for the future of the global economy. A fourth distinction of this work is that we recognize the ecological dimension to our present debt-monetary order. The ecological dimension can be stated thus: *the creation of money as interest-bearing debt is the motive force triggering the need for economic growth and an automatic progression in the destruction, despoliation, and commodification of the natural world of limited and finite resources*. A final difference with our work from that of Graeber is that we offer solutions to the problems discussed in the book. Not knowing exactly how to proceed with his research findings, Graeber more or less throws his hands up in the air at the end of his study.[16] Strangely, there is no proposed solution to some of the key problems he identifies other than praising the nonindustrious poor (2013: 390).[17] Our analysis, however, not only differs from Graeber's in the ways identified above but also offers feasible solutions that can be debated by activists and policymakers alike, and a strategy through which these reforms can be implemented.

Piketty's much-publicized work derives largely from over 200 years of data on wealth distribution, compiled by him and his associates, that shows that wealth and income inequality, high in the nineteenth century, fell in the mid-twentieth century, but has risen again and, according to Piketty, will continue to rise throughout the twenty-first century absent any measures to prevent it. *Capital* purports to explain the reasons for this wealth trajectory, and, implicitly the distribution and accumulation of power.

The key to his work relates to the relationship between the rate of return on capital (r) in an economy and its rate of economic growth (g). When the rate of return on capital, that is, financial return in the form of profits, dividends, interest, rents, royalties, and other incomes from capital, exceeds the rate of growth, that is, the national income, capitalism will automatically generate "arbitrary and unsustainable inequalities" that violate the meritocratic values at the foundation of democratic societies (Piketty 2014: 1). He represents this relationship as $r > g$. For example, in 1910 the income of the top 10 percent of the income distribution constituted some 45–50 percent of the national income, declined to under 35 percent in 1970, but rose again to 50 percent in 2007, declining slightly since then as a consequence of the 2007/2008 recession. Thus, since 1980, the top 10 percent of the income distribution appropriated three-quarters of income growth, the richest 1 percent received 60 percent, while the bottom 90 percent received less than 0.5 percent a year (Piketty 2014: 297). The same picture is true regarding wealth distribution. The top 10 percent, which owned between 60 and 80 percent of the wealth in the early nineteenth century, had its share of national wealth reduced to around 60 percent in the mid-twentieth century but now holds between 60 and 70 percent. In essence, Piketty demonstrates that the portion of national income that is owed to capital, that is, the return of profits, dividends, interest, rents, royalties, and so on, inexorably increases and presently claims some 30 percent of national income.

There are a number of reasons why wealth and income distribution converged in the mid-twentieth century according to Piketty, but according to him the major factors were the two world wars and the Great Depression, which not only destroyed capital but also prompted governments to formulate economic policies that increased labor's share of the national income. Absent these shocks to capital and the subsequent reversal of government policies regarding public spending, wealth and income inequality have again diverged, creating the inequalities we see today.

Piketty's arguments are, obviously, more complex and require consideration of such things as the role of inherited wealth in the economy and the role of the rise of what he calls "super-managers" and their outsized salaries, and we will be addressing some of Piketty's findings throughout this book, but at this point it is useful to highlight aspects of his work that relate most directly to ours.

While Piketty does not address debt, *per se* (there is no index entry), the book is every bit as much about debt as is Graeber's. Simply put, for the economic books to balance, for every capital investment, that is, for every expected return on capital, whether it be in the form of a loan, rent, a stock purchase, a business investment, and so on, there must be a corresponding debt and someone or something that will generate the return. This has a number of important implications.

First, it essentially divides society into net creditors and net debtors. The difference between these two analytical categories is that some— the net creditors—receive more income from capital than they pay out, while others—the net debtors—pay out more in interest than they receive. By recognizing this division between net creditors and net debtors (as opposed to simply viewing it abstractly as "capital" or "return on capital"), we get a better sense of the extent to which the vast majority of the population must generate financial returns for a small minority.

The second major point to extract from Piketty's work is the fact that while capital has a present existence it is always future oriented, since the returns on capital are contingent on meeting present profit expectations in the future. In other words, the great unknown is whether returns on capital can be realized. Recall that the total global debt in 2014 was $199 trillion; while we don't know exactly the expected return on that debt, nor the time period in which it must be paid, we do know that if future economic growth is insufficient, there can be dire consequences. Regardless, the future owes a debt to the present; capital has a claim on the future (or, as Piketty puts it, "the past devours the future") and the size of that claim obviously makes a big difference. Regardless, if, as Piketty shows, historical precedent is any indicator, capital will exercise a greater and greater claim on future income, and the question is whether economic growth will be sufficient to meet that claim, and, if not, where will capital attempt to realize or seize its expected return?

And this takes us to a third major point of Piketty's work: growth, he predicts, will slow and approach the historical average of 1.5–2 percent, while expected return on capital will remain at its historic average of 4–6 percent. Piketty doesn't explain, as we will try to do, why growth will slow, recognizing only that the growth rates of emerging economies will slow to that of rich countries, a phenomenon that economists refer to as "convergence"; but economists do recognize that the wealthier a country becomes, the more difficult increasing the rate of growth will be. But this fact has enormous import given the present and growing claim of capital, that is, creditors, on national income. So, what are the main factors inhibiting growth and the ability of the future to repay the past or debtors to repay creditors? We'll mention only two here.

First, economic growth is exponential, such that an economy growing at a 3 percent rate must essentially double every twenty-three years. Thus, if the global economy grew at 3 percent a year, by 2100, as we will see, it would approach a quadrillion dollars. We will examine this limitation on growth in more detail in Chapter 4.

Second, economic growth is largely dependent on fossil fuel energy and this type of energy is a nonrenewable resource that is likely to increase in cost throughout the twenty-first century. In fact, our economy is essentially based on the transformation of energy (largely from fossil fuels but other sources as well) into money, and either a decline in the availability of energy or an increase in its cost will substantially hinder continued growth. In other words, our societies monetize energy flows and stores. While Piketty basically ignores the role of energy in the economy, as does Graeber, it may be no accident that the historical period of convergence of income corresponds to the period of plentiful and affordable oil.

If, then, the rate of growth slows, but capital investments, and consequently its inverse—debt—grows, how can capital's share of the national income be honored and defaults, bankruptcies, and financial chaos avoided? This is where the full consequences of debt as a technology of power can be appreciated.

If more and more income is owed to capital, which is almost all in private hands, and if the power of capital and debt supersedes all others, then capital's claim on future income will trump all other claims, regardless of moral or humanitarian consequences, a point that Graeber emphasizes. As we have seen in the past thirty years, and more recently during the economic contraction of 2007/2008, the claims of capital or creditors were the first honored, even if that required taxpayer bailouts, or the taking of money from other public resources (e.g., education health and welfare) or from labor's share of the national income. Quantitative easing is also a way in which the central banks in the capitalist core have tried to re-inflate the capital markets.

Unlike Graeber, who offers no solution, Piketty is far bolder. According to him, the only way we can avoid the problem is through a global tax on wealth. This, he says, will lower the claim of capital on national wealth and provide funds to minimize the damage. Such a utopian solution, he says, can only be accomplished through banking laws that make wealth holdings transparent. A number of countries, including Italy, Spain, and Sweden, have attempted this. The problem, as Italy discovered, is that without international laws, capital will simply flee to friendlier havens to escape the tax. The difficulty, of course, is persuading governments to consider such measures and examine whether this is the only solution, an issue we will return to in Chapter 5.

Arguments and structure

As a technology of differential social power, debt is intertwined with
local and global social struggles with interconnected and international
implications for the future of the global economy. This book makes a
series of interrelated arguments around this general claim. First, debt,
and its inverse credit, can be theorized as a major technology of power
known by its effects on social relations and environmental change.
The main purpose of debt has not been so much to enable debtors;
instead it has been, more importantly, to disable them from engaging
in certain practices that would find them outside the orbit of the world
market of differential accumulation. Capitalist debt helps to produce
market-based subjects (Mahmud 2012: 469). Second, as the institution
of exclusive private property advanced by violence and legal sanction,
debt was mobilized in a more systematic and intensified manner by
those in the control of credit in order to shape and reshape the terrain
of social reproduction for the sake of the symbolic accumulation of
power represented in money. Third, there is a transition to the modern,
organized control of credit/debt with the birth of the national debt
and the extension and amplification of state bureaucracy, taxation,
standing armies, and over time, the *private* capitalization of banking or
money creation. Fourth, by the twentieth century, credit/debt largely
becomes depersonalized and corporatized so that a small number of
investors have come to capitalize evermore aspects of human endeavor
and natural resources through their ownership of banks and financial
instruments. Fifth, the present *magnitude* and *globalization* of debt
would not have been possible without the exploitation of abundant,
affordable, and accessible fossil fuels. In other words, the exploitation
of a surplus energy source permitted some of humanity to delink
themselves from the austerity of organic economies with lower
surpluses. However, as fossil fuel energy becomes evermore expensive
in the twenty-first century, we are likely to experience more intensive
debt crises at all levels of society and across political boundaries, as

more of people's disposable income is transferred to those in control of the energy that they require to socially reproduce their lifestyles. Sixth, modern money, created largely as interest-bearing debt, spurs the need for economic growth, with drastic social, cultural, and environmental consequences that are leading to evermore social dislocations and dire environmental consequences such as the loss of biodiversity, deforestation, desertification, and global climate change. Seventh, in the twentieth century, debt becomes more connected to a culture of materialism and conspicuous consumption, whereby people are encouraged and conditioned to self-actualize through the purchase of advertised commodities (Gill 1995). Eighth, current levels of debt imply what Polanyi called a "stark utopia": the belief that the modern system of money created as interest-bearing debt can continue *ad infinitum* on a finite planet. So long as our political and business leaders continue to cling to this false utopia of endless money-debt and growth, transitioning to a saner, more equitable, and environmentally sustainable world will be near impossible. Last, there is a need not only to interpret the present situation and to understand it historically but also to change it to ensure the well-being, if not the survival, of humanity. Moreover, for those who believe in democracy—that the people should have a say in their own governance— it is imperative that the public claims ownership over the control of money and manufacturers it in such a way that will avoid crippling debt and the redistribution of wealth upward. Building on the outcomes of our study, we offer a way in which this might be addressed through a Party of the 99% and a political strategy that uses debt itself as a means to promote change; we consider also how we might imagine ways of decapitalizing a near-universal but radically unequal sociality of debt that has emerged and intensified with the private capitalization of the power to create and allocate money as interest-bearing debt.

To examine these claims in more detail, we have organized the remainder of this book into four chapters organized by theme: the modern origins of capitalist debt, how debt as a technology of power was intensified historically, the consequences of modern debt, and what is to be done. We provide a brief summary of each to conclude this introduction.

In Chapter 2 we investigate the modern origins of debt as a technology of power by focusing on war, the creation of the "national" debt, and the capitalization of the organized force of the state. We trace the origins of debt as a technology of power to a confluence of events in seventeenth-century England. However, far from seeing this as a series of discrete events untainted by international interconnections, we theorize them as already embedded in a web of dynastic, geopolitical, and domestic relations of force. The purpose of founding the national debt in England—which was war—is already stamped with the financial machinations of the Dutch empire, Italian city-states of the fourteenth and fifteenth centuries, the Atlantic slave trade, and the conquest of North America and India by capitalized joint-stock companies such as the East India Company. The main argument in this chapter is that the invention of a funded long-term national debt was principally born not to finance wars to aggrandize the power of the Crown *per se* but more importantly to aggrandize the power of what Justin Rosenberg (1994) has called "the empire of civil society"—or to be more accurate, those members in civil society with the means and mentality to accumulate money, not the unpropertied, pauperized masses. The way we approach this account of the rise of debt as a technology of power is to understand it from the point of view of the powerful who came to capitalize the state by effectively owning *private shares* in the government's right to tax its citizenry (Marx 1887; Nitzan and Bichler 2009: 294ff). But since the state's primary function at this time was war-making, the capitalization of the state meant that investors were also capitalizing the ability of the state to mobilize its organized violence to quell domestic dissent and open and keep open colonies and trade routes. With this in mind, we must also be concerned to illustrate how the capitalization of joint-stock companies contributed to debt and the transformation of human relations and the environment as merchants pursued differential earnings outside of England, and after the Acts of Union (1707) in Britain.

In Chapter 3 we use the term "intensification" rather than spread or proliferation to think about both the amplification *and* spatial expansion of debt as a technology of power during the era of European colonialism and resistance. Once again we start from the point of view of the powerful—of superior force and violence in the quest for differential accumulation. Here, we examine how imposing imperial taxation regimes or what we call "imperial monetization" (always backed by force and punishment) contributed to displacing modes of life not connected up with the international market of price and profit. Unlike Graeber and Braudel, we do not see the market as something separate from capitalism but the very *precondition* for the emergence of capitalization and debt as a technology of power (Nitzan and Bichler 2009). As numeric computational power processes, capitalization and debt can only work through price, and where contracts, transactions, activities, and so forth cannot be priced, bought, and sold, capitalization and debt as technology of power cannot operate. Put another way, the market is not a space outside of capitalization or debt but the chief enabling mechanism for the accumulation of differential power represented in money. We then move to examine how "national" debts were created and administered in the colonies, the impact decolonization movements had on these historical structures, and the major events leading up to the debt crisis of the 1980s in what today is referred to as the Global South. We conclude the chapter with an examination of the sovereign debt crisis in the so-called heartland of global capitalism or what Pettifor (2006) has called the "coming first world debt crisis."

In Chapter 4 we examine the consequences of debt as a technology of power at both the macrolevel (e.g., environmental destruction, inequality of wealth, and life chances) and microlevel (e.g., the re-emergence of debtor prisons in the United States and the disciplining of indebted subjects). With these two levels in mind, we explore three major consequences of the private capitalization of money as interest-bearing debt.

The first major consequence is that the creation of money as debt requiring interest requires evermore economic growth and therefore the greater and more rapid exploitation of natural resources. There are three chief obstacles to this pursuit, and why continuing to believe the present system can replicate itself in perpetuity implies blatant utopic thinking: (1) the planet is finite and we are exhausting many of our resources at an accelerated pace, (2) fossil fuels are nonrenewable and their combustion contributes excessively to global warming/dimming, and (3) there has never been an example of continuous exponential growth on earth.

A second consequence is that our creation of money through loans/debt, where the interest is never created, means that there is always more debt in the system than there is the ability to repay it. For example, when a bank extends a loan of $1,000 dollars at 10 percent interest, it does not create the money to pay that interest—which would be $100. Put simply, the bank creates $1,000 not $1,100. So the question must be, where the interest comes from? The only possible solution is that the interest must come from the principal itself—meaning there is never enough money in the system to clear all debts. In this sense, the source of debt as a technology of power for creditors lies in its very permanence.

A third consequence is the intensification of neoliberalism and austerity measures in various countries experiencing higher levels of debt to GDP ratios, not to mention capital flight and tax evasion (e.g., Greece). Here we examine the impact of austerity measures and the growth of debt levels and how they affect citizens of indebted nations as well as those in developed countries. We will also re-examine Thomas Piketty's work and suggest that he neglects to consider the role of debt in the increasing income and wealth gaps that he documents, and we will illustrate the extent to which debt serves as a device of wealth transfer. Finally, to demonstrate the extent to which debt as a technology of power has colonized our lives, we'll examine the question of who, under the existing political economy, controls our future.

Having considered the consequences of debt as a technology of power in Chapter 4, in Chapter 5 we examine what should and can be done about debt in the current conjuncture. Our first argument is that a Party of the 99% with a specific party platform is a useful starting point for thinking about resistance to the present debt order. Our second argument focuses on using debt itself to force the decapitalization of the present monetary order so that a small minority cannot capitalize the labor of others or the world's natural resources for their own symbolic accumulation. In this regard, it is important to realize that, while debt is a technology of power, and that creditors exercise an inordinate amount of control over debtors, the wealth of the 1% lies largely in the pockets of the 99% where it must work to generate ever-increasing returns for the dominant owners of capital.

Origins: War, National Debt, and the Capitalized State

The initiators of the modern credit system take as their point of departure not an anathema against interest-bearing capital in general, but on the contrary, its explicit recognition. (Marx 1981: 429)

In order to trace how debt became a technology of organized differential social power under capitalism and the consequences this technology has on social relations and the environment, we must provide a brief genealogy of its emergence. Due to disciplinary silos and the prevalence of contested concepts across disciplines, we are in immediate danger of falling into traps if we are not clear what we are looking for at the outset. Many mainstream scholars of money, finance, and the capitalist firm try to convince us that capitalism has primarily been about the mitigation of risk, decreasing transaction costs, organizational and technological efficiency, and equilibrium prices (Roy 1997). In this reading of history, it is as if the goal of all human evolution—the *telos* of the species—has been the reduction of risk and transaction costs, the search for greater efficiency, and the endless search for equilibrium prices and Pareto optimality. We do not deny some role for these phenomena and fetishes—real or imaginary. What we do not share is this teleological approach to historical inquiry. First, because it occludes the illegitimate hierarchical effects of organized power and second because our starting point of differential power relations does not permit a teleological reading of history. In short, things can always be otherwise, and part of our task as scholars is to uncover how the present is no natural or progressive derivation, but constituted in social struggles that simultaneously

open up and close down political prospects. But an antiteleological
view, skeptical of progressive or linear renderings of history, does not
mean that history is absent human logic and rational pursuits.[1] As
Weatherford has argued, "every culture organizes life around a few
simple principles, activities and beliefs" (1997: 8). Without wanting to
minimize other aspects of human endeavor, in *capitalist* culture, life
and social reproduction are largely organized, we contend, around the
logic of differential accumulation and the ritual of capitalization in an
effort to gain more money and power over others and the environment
(Nitzan and Bichler 2009). This is the pathological pursuit not of the
entire population—who generally pursue what could be called the *logic
of livelihood*—but only of a small minority. In other words, most people
pursue money because they need it to survive and have a decent quality
of life, not as an end in itself and not always to exert power over others.
At the center of this order stands the privileged subject of capitalist
history: the investors or capitalists who are driven by their own logic
to accumulate differentially (Gill 1995). Differential accumulation
simply means that capitalists aim to accumulate more money faster
than others relative to a moving benchmark or shifting "normal" rate of
return. In this sense, capitalists have no idea what maximum profits are,
since they can only assess their performance relative to other capitalists
trying to do the exact same (Nitzan and Bichler 2009: 241 and 309).
For example, if I make 5 percent returns on my investments over a year
and you make 7 percent, I know that my decisions were inferior relative
to yours. If the average return on investment, however, is 11 percent,
then both of us have drastically underperformed even those who have
achieved "average" returns. If we were serious about beating the average
rate of return, then our underperformance would be an indication that
we need to change strategies.

The concept of capitalization is closely related to the logic of
differential accumulation. Capitalization is the act of investors
discounting a future flow of income into a present value adjusted
by some factor of risk. The exact math, along with the time value
theory of money, took a while to develop, but as we will see, the act
of discounting future profit flows based on some assessment of risk

has a long historical pedigree.[2] As we know from Chapter 1, most capitalization consists of some form of debt instrument, mostly various forms of government debt, financial bonds, and nonsecuritized loans (e.g., student loans and credit cards). The other way capitalization is accomplished is in the equity or stock market. These markets are historically novel and a way of organizing corporate power and ownership (Henwood 1997). They provide investors with an exit option should they want to sell their ownership claims to companies or buy new claims to the income streams of other firms. Worldwide outstanding capitalization is $67 trillion across sixty major exchanges.[3] Di Muzio (2014) has argued that the rise in capitalization from humble beginnings coincided with the exploitation of energy derived from fossil fuels.[4] Thus, what this suggests is that a key facet of capitalist culture since its emergence is the explosive rise in capitalization and institutions like the stock market, to support the trade in ownership claims over the future profit of companies shaping social reproduction by capitalizing energy. The largest companies in the world by market capitalization are called "dominant capital" by Nitzan and Bichler (2009). When we refer to "dominant capital," in this book we mean the companies listed on the Global *Financial Times* 500—a list of firms ranked by market capitalization.[5] These firms have tremendous power to shape and reshape patterns of social reproduction given their control over production and social reproduction. They control energy, food, medicine, clothing, software, media, telecommunications, transport, mineral wealth, and much more. It is also important to note that many of these nonfinancial firms are also deeply in debt to banks. For example, US nonfinancial corporate debt is $13.9 trillion according to the Federal Reserve.[6]

But while differential accumulation is the dominant logic of capitalism and capitalization its dominant ritual, market dependence and the price system are also integral to capitalism. This means that money—in this case, the unit of account—is absolutely central to capitalism since accumulation is measured in pecuniary terms and only pecuniary terms. Insofar as this is an accurate assessment of our affairs, we ought to have a clear understanding of how capitalist money is created. As Ingham and others have noted, there is considerable confusion over what money is and how it is produced. Orthodox economics is of no help. Modern economics textbooks continue to inculcate a distorted and incorrect account of modern money creation, leading to generations of graduates leaving school with little understanding of arguably the most important social institution of their societies. As Ingham has explained and others have confirmed, modern money is "a social relation of credit and debt denominated in a money of account" (2004: 12; see also Rowbotham 1998). The majority of any country's money supply is produced when banks issue loans to willing borrowers, namely, governments, businesses, and households.[7] In other words, banks are not intermediaries—they do not take from savers and lend to borrowers with differential interest rates.[8] Nor does the creation of money depend upon someone entering a commercial bank to make a deposit (Sheard 2013). Commercial banks are quite simply "merchants of debt" that produce and allocate needed money as interest-bearing debt (Minsky cited in Ingham 2004: 161).

In traditional economic accounts, money is said to play at least three roles in society: a medium of exchange, a store of value, and a unit of account or measure of value. Following Innes and Keynes, Ingham (2004) argues that the unit of account function of money is far more important than the actual role played by the "medium" of exchange (Wray 2004). Money is not paper bills, coins, gold, silver, or chocolate, but an abstract unit of account that can be represented by any medium (albeit, the medium is typically selected by a political authority or power-holder and must meet certain standards). As Ingham (2004) and others argue, the role of money as an abstract measure of value is logically and historically prior to any fascination with coins or the gold standard and can at least be traced back to the first agrarian command economies of the Nile and Tigris (Wray 2004). Indeed, as Rowbotham suggests, "most money exists purely as a number" (1998: 10). However, while we should not confuse money with a "thing" or a material substance as do most mainstream economists, Ingham argues that we can conceive of four historical modes of monetary production:

- Money accounting according to a standard of value without transferrable tokens (earliest known case: Mesopotamia, third millennium BC)
- Precious metal coinage systems (Asia Minor, ca. 700 BC to early twentieth century AD)
- Dual system of precious metal coinage and credit-money (fifteenth to early twentieth century)
- The pure capitalist credit-money system (mid-twentieth century onwards) (Ingham 2004: 77–78).

We agree with Schumpeter, Keynes, and Ingham that one of the key aspects that distinguishes capitalism from earlier forms of organizing society and its endeavors is the way in which money is created as interest-bearing debt (Schumpeter citied in Ingham 2004: 63). If, as Nitzan and Bichler (2009) claim, capital is commodified differential social power measured in money, then we ought to be highly curious how money is produced and allocated in our societies. In this chapter we argue that the key to understanding debt as a technology of power is not just to appreciate that modern money is largely created as debt by commercial banks but to point out, more importantly, that the production and allocation of money is *privately owned*. Thus, to provide a genealogy of debt as a technology of power in this chapter, we must be concerned with how the production and allocation came to be privately owned, controlled, and capitalized by the few. The corollary of this social fact is not simply that it makes the relationship between debtors and creditors paramount in capitalism but that the supply of money is "subject to rigorous control" so that there is always a demand for money and a dearth of its availability (Rowbotham 1998; Ingham 2004: 7). To use Veblen's language, we could call the private ownership over the production and allocation of money the greatest "sabotage" in human history since, in order to exert any power whatsoever, the owners of banks and their managers must effectively incapacitate or restrict the money supply and war against possible alternatives to their effective monopoly. So far they have been very successful because they have attached themselves to state power. One indication is that money and monetary reform were very heavily debated in the past (Rowbotham 1998: 7). Today, debates and proposals for monetary reform do occur, but they are relatively marginal and have so far failed to gain significant political traction despite the obvious unfairness and frailty of the current system of modern finance and money production. This is what makes debt a technology of differential power beneficial to creditors: private ownership over an exclusive right to create credit (money as debt) and, over time, the naturalization of this power as private—both feats strongly assisted by the fact that most mainstream economics textbooks teach a completely inaccurate model of how money is supplied to the economy (Häring 2013). But while this is a central aspect of our argument, we also recognize that what is ultimately being monetized and capitalized is energy in its various forms. The money supply of various countries—particularly of the empires of England/Britain and later the United States—was allowed to expand because of surplus energy provided by fossil fuels. A further impetus of the present system of money creation, we argue, requires constant economic growth that is unsustainable in the long run due to the natural limits of some resources and the fact that fossil fuels—the primary source of energy for capitalism—are nonrenewable. It is worthwhile here to stop to consider why economic growth is so paramount to our societies. Why must our economies grow—even when GDP tells us nothing about human well-being (Daly 2005; Fioramonti 2013)?[9] It seems that there are at least three main reasons: two are imperative given the enforced scarcity of money for the majority and one is ideological. As identified by Rowbotham (1998: 37ff), forced economic growth first results from the competition for money to pay down debt or for use in buying goods and services. Since banks create money when they extend loans to borrowers *but do not create the interest*, there is always more debt in the system than there is the ability to repay the debt. For example, as stated above, business or nonfinancial corporate debt in the United States is $13.9 trillion. If we apply a simple rate of interest of just 3 percent, at the end of the year, the US business community would owe $417 billion to their creditors. Since this $417 billion has not been created at the time when the loans were taken out (the principal is only created, never the interest), the money to pay down business debt must be found elsewhere in the economy—thus ultimately removing it from popular circulation when debts are repaid. This creates a further scarcity of money in the economy. Moreover, the cost of borrowing must also be pushed on to consumers: it becomes an integral part of business pricing and inflation in the economic battle to accumulate differentially. Figure 2.1 demonstrates the rise in business debt in the United States and we assume a similar trajectory for other advanced capitalist nations.

The second factor identified by Rowbotham is the chronic lack of purchasing power in the economy, which results from the fact that "distributed incomes" are insufficient to purchase the goods and services produced in society. The evidence for this claim is the mounting consumer debt in rich countries. As *The Economist* reports, "The ratio of debt to disposable income rose by an average of 30 percentage points, to 130%, in OECD countries between pre-boom 2000 and pre-crisis 2007."[10] There would be no need for this consumer

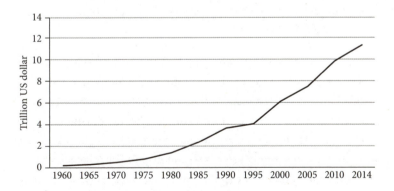

Figure 2.1 US nonfinancial business debt 1960–2014 Q1

Source: Federal Reserve, LA144104005. Q.

debt if there were not a chronic lack of purchasing power in the economy. Furthermore, even if everyone "lived within their means" or "only spent what they earned" as conservative social forces are wont to advocate, the global economy would inevitably collapse. For example, the total outstanding unsecured debt as of 2012 stood at $62 trillion dollars across 183 countries (McKinsey 2013). It is the *largest category of debt*—bigger than the total national debt of all countries combined— and is up by 170 percent from 1990. Such debt consists of personal loans, lines of credit, credit cards, and student debt among other debt "products." Now imagine if all of a sudden this debt-money vanished from the global economy. Disaster would surely ensue.

The third reason for forced economic growth is ideological insofar as the promise of economic growth is supposed to increase the wealth of everyone over time as the economic pie gets larger. Hence, political elites and the extremely wealthy avoid any clarion calls for redistribution or a transformation of the prevailing social relations of production and exchange. As Kempf argued,

> To escape any re-evaluation, the oligarchy keeps repeating the dominant ideology according to which the solution to the social crisis is production growth. That is supposedly the sole means of fighting poverty and unemployment. Growth would allow the overall level of wealth to rise and consequently improve the lot of the poor without— and this part is never spelled out—any need to modify the distribution of wealth. (2008: 70)

The need for economic growth in spite of observable ecological limits on a finite planet is thus hardwired into debt-based economies—it is encoded not only in the math of the system but also in the ideological politics of growth. To illustrate how pathological the pursuit of growth is, try imagining any politician running a successful campaign at present by arguing the need to degrow the economy. Or imagine a corporate chieftain arguing that he or she would like to generate fewer earnings in the next quarter than the last. Both are absurdities in a debt-based monetary system based on differential power.

So to sum up here, our brief genealogy of debt as a technology of power has to take account of the following:

- Differential accumulation
- The rise of capitalization based on fossil fuel energy
- Differences in modes of money production
- The creation of the price system and market dependence
- The ownership and capitalization of money production as interest-bearing debt
- The fact that debt-premised economies require perpetual economic growth
- The international dimensions of these phenomena.

To do so, we now turn to examine how debt became capitalized by organized power and find its genealogy rooted in war, the national debt, and the capitalized state of England.

Money, war, and debt before the Bank of England

While the social relations of credit and debt existed long before the emergence of capitalism, and money has taken many forms historically, we are interested in how debt became a technology of organized and capitalized power (Weatherford 1997; Davies 2002; Graeber 2011). The key development occurs with the creation of the Bank of England in 1694 and the innovation of a funded long-term national debt capable of being serviced by the ever-growing regressive taxation on the public (Dickson 1967; O'Brien 1988; Brewer 1989; Braddick 1996). But we should not theorize England as existing in isolation from the geopolitics, foreign markets, and the religious and dynastic power struggles of Europe and later, the world (Teschke 2009). As many scholars have observed, since the Norman Conquest of 1066, rulers actively centralized political power earlier than most continental nations (Wood 2002). Over time, the nobility was largely demilitarized relative to their continental counterparts, making violent challenges to centralized royal authority less likely (Brewer 1989). England also achieved the "first uniform national currency" by 1066—a feat that would take continental powers hundreds of years more to achieve (Davies 2002: 130). Finally, due to an "energy crisis" in the 1500s resulting from widespread deforestation that priced wood out of reach for many, more of England's population turned to coal as a key source of energy (Nef 1977; Sieferle 2010). This new energy source and the need to excavate more coal from the watery bowels of the earth sparked what has popularly been called the world's first Industrial Revolution as steam power and rail were used to pump water out of mines to extract and transport more coal energy (Smil 1994). As we will discuss briefly below, this new energy source inspired a number of inventions and innovations, increased productivity and surplus, and ignited the rise in British capitalization on the London Stock Exchange.

Despite these differences, England shared at least four characteristics with the nations of continental Europe. First, the country was overwhelming agrarian, undemocratic, and run for the benefit of royal authority and the lords of estates. Second, money was understood to be gold and silver rather than, say, pure credit or cattle. One of the chief goals of the rulers was to control the production of this money where possible and obtain evermore of it. Third, there was a dearth of money due to the belief that money could only be silver and gold—metallic substances believed to have some "intrinsic" worth. As a consequence, increasing the money supply could only be done in one of three ways: finding new mines at home or abroad, trading goods and services with other nations in exchange for gold and silver, or plundering it from others. Fourth, due to England's geography, it avoided much of the constant and expensive warfare experienced on the continent in the early modern era. However, England too engaged in foreign battles and was therefore in constant need of money to finance its conquests and conflicts and to satisfy the desire of its ruling class for more money, wealth, and power (Brewer 1989).

Up until the Glorious Revolution of 1688 and the creation of the Bank of England (1694) and the national debt, the production or creation of money and its initial allocation was the prerogative of the sovereign (Davies 2002: 136). The sovereign would enlist various "moneyers" or mint-masters of a certain reputation to mint the sovereign coins and occasionally remint them when they had become debased or overused. Minting errors or chicanery with the currency was greeted with corporeal punishment such as the chopping off of hands, blinding, or castration, if not all three acts (Davies 2002: 140). These coins would then be spent into the economy, particularly for war-making or the support of soldiers in continental battles for dynastic power and wealth. This created a situation where private merchants engaged in the production and trade of goods and services could potentially amass a small fortune in coins. It is also worth remembering that the historical record appears to confirm that, at least in the early modern era before the Industrial Revolution, most peasants had little access to this form of money (Dyer 1997; Gilbert and Helleiner 1999: 3). In other words, metallic money of the silver and gold variety was circulated by the powerful in pursuit of their interests as an early form of accounting for their social power to command goods and services from others (Davies 2002: 145). Money was largely a product of the powerful, not a weapon of the weak. Some of the coins spent into the economy by the regent would then be redistributed to the sovereign purse through official taxation. This meant that monetary and fiscal policies were tightly linked. As Davies noted, "minting and taxing were two sides of the same coin of royal prerogative" (2002: 147). Taxation made the coins valuable since they were needed to pay taxes.

However, unlike royal authority in France, which was constantly on the prowl for more taxes because it had to pay for a burgeoning group of venal officeholders who were often tax exempt themselves, English sovereigns appear to have been more constrained by their subjects. This made it more difficult to overburden the population with excessive taxes—particularly without regular parliaments. This does not mean that taxes were not onerous on some populations; it is just to suggest that from a comparative perspective, the English were more lightly taxed than their counterparts in France, with the burden falling more on the propertied than on the nonmonetized peasantry. However, after the Glorious Revolution of 1688 and the creation of the national debt, the English would become the most heavily taxed population in all of Europe. As we will discuss momentarily, a plethora of new taxes was raised to finance the English ruling class's continental wars and colonial conquests (O'Brien 1988; Brewer 1989). But this could not have had any effect and, indeed, would have destroyed the economy without an expansive monetary supply first occasioned by the Bank of England issuing loans originally backed by silver coinage (Carruthers 1996; Davies 2002; Wennerlind 2011).

What is often forgotten is that before the sovereign was made subordinate to Parliament, financing war was the *personal* responsibility of royal authority. With relatively strict limits placed upon taxation, and with a limited money supply, this meant that if the sovereign wanted to pay for expensive wars, he or she could only raise funds in a limited number of ways. First, the sovereign could borrow from private subjects and where finance was not forthcoming, the regent could force loans. The first option was limited by the creditor's perception of the royal finances, while the second (forced loans) was limited by the private power of moneyed lenders and their ability to obscure their truth worth. Second, peerage titles, venal offices, monopolies, and royal lands could be sold for ready cash to private social forces. While the first two options were not as common as the practice was in France, the third and fourth options (discussed below) were very common and a chief source of royal revenue. In fact, since Richard I (1189–99), successive monarchies effectively "privatized" royal assets and privileges when they needed money to repay debts and/or finance war (Davies 2002: 158; Wennerlind 2011: 25). Brewer put this in the context of war:

> The fiscal demands of the crown also prompted the sale of trade privileges and monopolies. Joel Hurstfield has described this as "putting up for auction the machinery of government itself." Begun by Elizabeth and rapidly expanded during the Spanish War in the

1580s and 1590s, the practice reached a peak in the 1630s when the monopolies on starch, coal, salt and soap raised £80,000 a year for the crown, and between £200,000 and £300,000 for the monopolists. (1989: 14)

As we shall see, this practice of selling state assets to repay debt continues to this day. The only difference is that "public" rather than "royal" assets are now sold to private capitalists—a key facet of debt being mobilized as a technology of the powerful in our own times (Chossudovsky 2002: 55ff; Perkins 2004). A third way regents could raise funds was from rents on the royal estates. This was a key source of revenue, but since successive regents sold off more and more royal property, the proceeds were never sufficient to finance war and other affairs of state. A fourth option was to debase the currency by lessening its metallic content, thus creating more coins out of the same metallic base. This was, of course, a highly contested option among the true believers in sound metallic money. Two additional avenues could be used: the plunder of gold and silver from enemies and, by the time of Henry VIII, the dissolution of the monasteries. The expropriation and private sale of the monasteries was primarily a revenue-raising exercise as the "department established to supervise the dissolution, the Court of the Augmentation of the Revenues of the King's Crown" makes clear (Woodward 1966; Davies 2002: 194ff).

So what are we to make of money, war, and debt before the Bank of England? First, while the sovereign did have the ability to mint money, once it was spent into the economy, successive regents lost control of it and could only recollect money through taxation and the various other means mentioned above. What this suggests is that while the regent was effectively above the law and therefore exercised differential legal power over subjects, at base the regent had *very limited financial power*. The way in which money was spent into the economy, private monopolies were granted, and royal assets were sold allowed private social forces to amass greater and greater fortunes ultimately giving a small group of merchants and creditors considerable financial power over the juridically superior monarch. Second, at least since Richard I, all successive monarchies were in constant debt to creditors, which continued to weaken their power over time. Evidence of this can be seen in the emergent political theory of the time. Harrington's tract *Oceana* (1656) argued that the breakdown of the monarchy in the bloody English Civil Wars (1642–51) was largely the result of a shift in the financial power of the propertied (Pipes 1999: 32). Differential power in property and finance now rested with wealthy subjects rather than the monarch. The regent could not be all powerful and the nation's largest debtor at the same time. Third, the fiscal demands of the sovereign were largely for the purposes of war-making and defending the realm—expensive propositions that called for evermore money (Brewer 1989). Last, because money was primarily thought of as silver and gold, there was virtually always a scarcity of money, though not of potential material capacity (Davies 2002: 170). Increasing the money supply meant debasement or finding new sources of silver and gold by trading with other nations, plundering other nations, or finding and exploiting new mines. If the monarch would have had the power to create capitalist credit-money out of thin air, the history of capitalism might have been radically different. But rather than becoming the realm's chief creditor, successive monarchies were typically the kingdom's chief debtors. In this light, it is hardly surprising that the regent would eventually be made subordinate to the financially prosperous and propertied in Parliament. As it turns out, the power to create money as interest-bearing debt was given to private social forces. Thus, a potentially public institution operating in the interests of all emerged as a private institution operating in the interests of a small class of merchants and financiers.

The Old Lady of Threadneedle Street

By the time of the Glorious Revolution of 1688—a revolution that solidified parliamentary power over the monarchy—elite debates had raged over the scarcity of money and what could be done about the dire situation. Moreover, there was a general feeling among certain sectors of the elite that the economy was not living up to its full potential. Capacity to improve and produce more agricultural goods and manufactures seemed within technical reach, but so long as money was conceptualized as bullion, the supply could not be easily increased and expanding commerce beyond a certain limit, virtually impossible. As Wennerlind notes, "while modern economic theory does not recognize the possibility of a scarcity of money, seventeenth-century thinkers were *consumed* by this problem" (2011: 17 our emphasis). In an effort to expand the money supply, contemporaries even sought the philosopher's stone, or the alchemical ability to transform base metals into gold and silver. The idea of credit was well known and extensively used domestically and in international exchange, but like alchemy, it too was limited (Muldrew 1998). Before the Bank of England, credit was traditionally a private and personal affair between known lenders and borrowers—not a social relation among strangers. It is also true that goldsmiths extended the currency by issuing paper notes in excess of their gold deposits (Davies 2002: 249ff). But whatever the various types of credit notes or pledges in existence to facilitate commerce, they were neither generally assignable nor transferrable, thereby limiting their use as a normally circulating currency that could replace the national coinage in circulation and increase the supply of money with any great effect (Wennerlind 2011: 69).

In this atmosphere of scarce money, a hundred or more proposals were put forward for some type of public bank that could relieve the popular cry for more money (examined more fully in Horsefield 1960). On the heels of these proposals, only one scheme was officially sanctioned: the privately owned, for-profit Bank of England. As Dickson (1967) has argued, this institutional innovation ushered in a "financial revolution" that would facilitate the agricultural and industrial revolutions. However, as Wennerlind (2011) argues, what was ultimately required before any institution could be developed to solve the problem of scarce coinage was an epistemological revolution that dissociated money from a metallic substance such as gold or silver. Wennerlind traces this to the Hartlib Circle's belief in the possibility of constant improvement and their reinterpretation of money as a symbol of value rather than a staunch material substance. As he explains,

> The Hartlibians believed that by facilitating circulation and engendering productive endeavors, money had the capacity to activate hidden or dormant resources in nature and mankind. Money thus partnered with knowledge and industry as the key ingredients in the infinite expansion of nature and society. Moreover, as the world of goods expanded continuously the money stock had to be able to grow proportionally in order to circulate all the new commodities ... Expanding the money stock was therefore no longer about solving a temporary scarcity of money, but rather about the introduction of a monetary mechanism that could facilitate change and growth, *ad infinitum*. (2011: 45)

This ideological transformation, however, did not wholly delink credit from a metallic substance—a mode of money production not countenanced *fully* until the United States abandoned the gold standard instituted by the Bretton Woods agreement of 1944. Nor, as is the case today, did this institutional innovation delink money from war or the preparation for war (albeit some states have smaller military budgets and a few, none at all, e.g., Costa Rica). In fact, while the birth of the Bank of England can be traced to the scarcity of money debates of the seventeenth century, the ultimate reason for its creation was not the Hartlibian improvement of society but to finance war against Europe's most powerful ruler, Louis XIV. As Davies makes clear,

> The Bank of England came into being by the Ways and Means Act of June 1694 and was confirmed by a Royal Charter of Incorporation (27 July 1694). The Act makes it clear that its real purpose was to raise money for the War of the League of Augsburg by taxation and by the novel device of a permanent loan, the bank being very much a secondary matter, though essential to guarantee the success of the main purpose. (2002: 259)

The political settlement of 1688 placed more power in the hands of Parliament to govern and oversee the fiscal matters of the realm. This gave greater confidence to city merchants, goldsmiths, and property holders more generally, who had often been the victims of forced loans, arbitrary taxation, and royal defaults in the past (North and Weingast 1989). Organized by the Scot, William Paterson, and a coterie of city merchants, the Bank of England was to extend a permanent loan of £1.2 million in banknotes to the new government to finance the war with France. In exchange, the bank received corporate existence, 8 percent annual interest on the initial sum lent (£100,000), and a £4000 pound annual management fee (Davies 2002: 260; Broz and Grossman 2004: 56). The income stream of interest and fees paid to the Bank of England was secured by a specific tax—the "Tonnage"—which raised taxes on the carrying capacity of sea-going vessels largely carrying alcohol. Together, these acts constituted a radical historical break from early forms of finance since, for the first time, a funded, permanent *national* debt was created. This meant that private creditors were no longer capitalizing the power of royal authority when they lent to the regent, but the fused power of the King-in-Parliament and their ability to tax the population by force if necessary. A further development stemming from this institutional innovation was that the money supply could be extended more fully than in the past. To recall, goldsmiths could issue their own notes in excess of their gold reserves, thus increasing the money supply. But this exercise was limited by their private reserves and the confidence of borrowers and depositors, and therefore individual goldsmiths could not solve the scarcity of money problem in England. What made the Bank of England unique was that it was an organized corporate force of creditors that capitalized the King-in-Parliament's power to tax, therefore guaranteeing a revenue stream of interest on a permanent public debt that would likely never be paid off in full.[11] Marx noticed the historical and international dimension of the public debt:

> The system of public credit, *i.e.*, of national debts, whose origin we discover in Genoa and Venice as early as the Middle Ages, took possession of Europe generally during the manufacturing period. The colonial system with its maritime trade and commercial wars served as a forcing-house for it. Thus it first took root in Holland.

National debts, *i.e.*, the alienation of the state—whether despotic, constitutional or republican—marked with its stamp the capitalistic era. The only part of the so-called national wealth that actually *enters into the collective possessions* of modern peoples is their national debt. Hence, as a necessary consequence, the modern doctrine that a nation becomes the richer the more deeply it is in debt. (1887: 529)

What made England different from its precursors is that backed up by a relatively small reserve of silver (and later gold), the Bank of England could also issue assignable notes in considerable excess of its reserves—effectively creating a new currency and expanding the money supply to greater effect than individual goldsmiths. As Wennerlind points out, though there were historical precursors, this created "England's and Europe's first widely circulating credit currency" (2011: 109).

Scholars of the "financial revolution" in England have made much of these developments since Dickson's (1967) seminal work on the Bank of England and the permanent national debt. However, despite minor disagreements in the literature, most have focused on the institutional factors that made the revolution a success. These scholarly accounts tend to be more celebratory than critical and they too often downplay the effects of class power and violence in the making of debt as a technology of institutionalized social power—a power wielded, we remind the reader, by minority social forces extending loans as interest. Our approach is different: we want to uncover the power underpinnings of this new relation of force between money-creating creditors and the majority of debtors. Not only do we want to uncover the international dimensions of this new institutional apparatus of credit, debt, and political power, but we also want to demonstrate the ways in which the exclusive nature of money creation as interest-bearing debt by private social forces was instantiated and the consequences of this system's operations on political economies today. We will discuss this in greater detail in the next two chapters, but here we want to draw out some of the key theoretical and practical dimensions of debt as a technology of power at its institutionalized inception.

First, the national debt backed by the government's power to tax facilitated colonial adventures and furthered wars that dispossessed first peoples of their land, enforced their labor and new ways of life, destroyed languages and culture, and put to death many of those who resisted imperial policy. All of this extended ruling-class power in Britain through the internationalization of debt relationships backed by superior force. As Brewer notes, "after 1688 the scope of British military involvement changed radically. Britain was at war more frequently and for longer periods of time, deploying armies and navies of unprecedented size" (1989: 22). Indeed, in the eighteenth century, English governments spent "between 75 percent and 85 percent of annual expenditure" on the military apparatus or servicing debts to private creditors for previous wars (Brewer 1989: 31). Thus, the so-called "national" debt was intimately tied up with ruling-class power and a growing apparatus of transformative international violence. But there is something more missed by most observers of this period. The power of money creation was slowly slipping toward private creditors at the Bank of England, and later commercial banks outside and inside of London, and this meant that financing the organized violence of ruling-class power embodied in the state was *the largest way in which new money entered the economy*. Put another way, as Britain's national debt ballooned to pay for wars, so too did its monetary supply and interest charges owed to private creditors.[12] With more war, there was more money in the economy and therefore the potential for greater prosperity, albeit unevenly shared across the class hierarchy. While the nature of national belligerence may have changed since the days of formal colonialism, government spending on war and the preparation for war is still one of the fundamental ways in which new money enters the economy. For example, at least since 2000 if not before, the United States current account deficit closely mirrors its defense spending so that if defense spending were significantly curtailed it is likely that the United States could achieve balance of payment surpluses (see Figure 2.2). Yet if this war-spending is not forthcoming or replaced by other types of government spending, the global money supply of

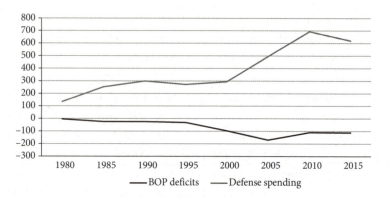

Figure 2.2 US military spending and current account deficit 1980–2014
Source: Federal Reserve and OMB. Historical Tables 3.2.

dollars (effectively the world's most important reserve currency) will contract and there will inevitably be more financial crises, business failures, and higher world unemployment. The "fiscal-military-state" or what some have called the welfare-warfare state is the direct result of debt being mobilized as a private technology of power (Clayton 1976; Brewer 1989).

Second, debt as a technology of power cannot be mobilized without exclusive ownership and the right to exclude others from doing the same thing. If everyone is a creditor, there are no debtors. Although the initial charter of the Bank of England did not grant the bank an exclusive monopoly over the issue of paper notes, as other social forces vied for the same power, the bank's owner-managers worked to solidify their exclusive rights. In the Bank of England's recharter of 1697, Parliament agreed that no other bank should be erected while the Bank of England remained in operation. As Parliament needed to finance more foreign wars, additional protections were included in renewed charters:

In 1708, during the War of Spanish Succession and again in exchange for a fresh loan, the Bank obtained from Parliament its most significant protection from competition: the legal prohibition of associations of more than six individuals from carrying on a banking business in

England. This was crucial in restricting competition, because issuing
bank notes was the major source of bank funding in this era. The Act
of 1708 thus gave the Bank a monopoly over joint-stock note issue.
(Broz and Grossman 2004: 57)

What this suggests is that early on, the bank sought to incapacitate
competing banks and secure its own exclusive rights to issue credit
to the government in return for political favors, interest, and fees. But
it was not just competing banks and ideas for releasing credit to the
public to facilitate trade that were attacked by the Bank of England's
operators. As Wennerlind's research shows, protecting the nascent
credit industry meant the death penalty for counterfeiters. To secure
the public's trust in credit, Sir Isaac Newton was made warden of the
mint and tasked with "investigating, detecting and prosecuting crimes
against the currency" (2011: 18). Since there could only be one real
counterfeiter—the Bank of England—members of the population who
clipped coins or counterfeited the new paper banknotes were punished
by death: hanging in the case of men and burning in the case of women
(Wennerlind 2011: 150). The death penalty was not only a monetary
policy but a deterrent for the inception of debt as a technology of
organized power (Wennerlind 2004). Today, the entire commercial
banking system depends on this type of exclusive right to issue credit
and the profits of these institutions are protected by a massive legal
apparatus that punishes crimes against money and sanctions what in
an earlier time used to be called usury (Geisst 2013). In most countries
today, usury is a legally sanctioned weapon of the powerful against the
weak. What this means is that not only do publically elected officials
actively refuse to create and allocate non-interest-bearing credit as a
public good, but they also enforce their very exclusion from money
creation! And while modern banking is not altogether a monopoly—
there is indeed ostensible competition among the banks for market
share—this is in considerable respects—illusory. Through interlocking
ownership, commercial banks have come to capitalize one another so
they have what could be called an "effective monopoly" on creating the
money supply (Vitali et al. 2011).

A third theoretical and practical dimension emerges from our brief analysis above: the relationship between differential capitalization, energy, and the normal rate of return. With the creation of the Bank of England and the national debt, a "normal" rate of return connected to state power was established.[13] Thus, at its inception, Parliament promised an 8 percent return on invested capital to city financiers who subscribed to the Bank of England. In modern parlance, this interest rate provided a "benchmark return" by which investors could judge alternative courses of investment, thus institutionalizing what Nitzan and Bichler (2009) call "differential accumulation" by pegging interest to state power. To this day, interest rates on government bonds remain the benchmark or heart of global finance since they all represent the state's power to tax its citizenry and service debt to creditors. Emerging alongside this market in government securities was the chartered joint-stock company (Scott 1912; Walker 1931; Micklethwait and Wooldrige 2003; Robins 2006). In England, these companies predate the Bank of England and were capitalized on the basis of their exclusive rights to profit from trade granted to them by royal charter. Yet two companies were particularly important for helping to finance or uphold the national debt of England: the South Sea Company and the East Indian Company. The South Sea Company was founded in 1711 and was originally intended to help alleviate government debt by engrafting government securities into company shares. The capitalization of the South Sea Company was largely contingent on the Spanish Asiento, which granted the company exclusive rights to sell African slaves to Latin America. In effect, investors who bought shares in the South Sea Company were betting on the profit and loss of the slave trade, or put differently, they were capitalizing the violence used to capture and commodify human life energy—a particularly important international dimension of England's ability to service its national debt to private social forces. The national debt also helped the East India Company finance its trade and colonial control of a considerable portion of Asia by using its ownership over some of the national debt to secure loans to finance its foreign operations (Baskin and Miranti 1997: 103). The Bank of England, the South Sea Company, and the East India Company had the largest capitalization of the time before more coal energy came on line to offer greater opportunities for capitalization in mines, steel, and railroads (Baskin and Miranti 1997: 56). In essence, by 1717, would-be equity investors had at least three *major* options to achieve differential accumulation: (1) they could capitalize the national debt and the power of the state to enforce domestic taxation and colonial policy; (2) they could invest in the slave trade to Latin America through the South Sea Company; and/or (3) they could invest in the gradual colonization and trade with Asia through the East India Company (Baskin and Miranti 1997: 56). These endeavors were immensely transformative and set the stage for the further development of debt as a technology of organized power. Nowhere was this perhaps more clear than in the colonies of Europe, where debt would gradually take over—but never wholly replace—the role of force in rendering the population useful for the differential accumulation of the few.

Intensification: War, Debt, and Colonial Power

If the history of progress has been written as a history of the emergence of the autonomous, possessive and self-possessed individual, it was the history of indebtedness that underlay this teleology. The latter history has subsisted in the shadow of forgetfulness.... (Banerjee 2000: 423)

The technology of debt was internationalized long before the state's power to tax was capitalized on the basis of a permanent national debt. As we saw in Chapter 2, the key rupture with the past was the creation of the Bank of England and the *permanent* national debt that stretched English money beyond the limitations of gold and silver coinage. The move also anchored the emergence of an international credit system based on sterling and the capitalization of colonialism. The new paper currency issues remained linked to a metallic substance during this period, but the tether was extended so that the value of paper notes in circulation was never fully backed by the metallic horde at the Bank of England and other provincial banks that would spring up during the Industrial Revolution. With varying degrees of success, this institutional innovation was later adopted by other nations that remained free of colonial rule. It helped to mitigate (never totally solve) the scarcity of money problem that had so riddled England and much of the European continent in an era of colonial plunder, slavery, long-distance trade, and the exploitation of a new energy source, that is, coal. The perpetual debt became a way of permanently locking in the relationship between private creditors and the power of the state to regulate commercial relations, tax its population, fight foreign wars, and quell domestic rebellion during a tumultuous time of social transformation and resistance. It also guaranteed a "normal rate of return" to capital since the ownership of government debt was assumed to be a far safer investment than risking one's money in foreign trade. As Marx understood,

> As with the stroke of an enchanter's wand, [the public debt] endows barren money with the power of breeding and thus turns it into capital, without the necessity of its exposing itself to the troubles and risks inseparable from its employment in industry or even in usury. The state creditors actually give nothing away, for the sum lent is transformed into public bonds, easily negotiable, which go on functioning in their hands just as so much hard cash would. (1887: 529)

In other words, not only did the public debt of nations become the key benchmark and the heart of a growing credit industry but investors never truly gave anything away since they could always sell their claim onto others or borrow based on the fact that their bonds were an asset. If not, they collected their money back with interest over time. As Ferguson (2006) has demonstrated, owning a small share of state power through government bonds was a lucrative enterprise during this era and one of the key routes to the accumulation of a private fortune. The Rothschilds are an extreme case in point, but they were not the only beneficiaries of "national" debts accumulated to fund wars (Ferguson 1998). However, while the benefits of holding government debt were not simply the purview of well-known historical capitalists, ownership—like financial knowledge—was still heavily skewed toward the few. According to Ferguson, "as a percentage of the population of England and Wales, bondholders were … a tiny and dwindling élite: from 2.7 percent of the population when Napoleon I was defeated to just 0.9 percent when the same fate befell Napoleon III" (2006: 195). As Ferguson notes, since the debt was largely funded by regressive forms of taxation, servicing the interest on the public debt represented "an astonishingly inequitable system of transfers from the poor majority to the bondholding minority" (2006: 195).

In this chapter we aim to historically illustrate both the amplification and spatial expansion of debt as a technology of power during the era of European colonialism and resistance and how this legacy extends to the present day. By starting from the point of view of the powerful—of superior force and violence in the quest for differential accumulation— we want to demonstrate how networks of indebtedness reconfigured political communities for the benefit of creditors and capitalists and how this continued on after formal colonialism started to come to an end in fits and starts after the Second World War. Over time, arguably, debt has become a more effective tool of wealth transfer and social transformation than war—though, of course, the two are intertwined in complex ways as the origins of the permanent public debt in England make clear. Since we cannot hope to provide a comprehensive study in such a short volume, what we intend to do is examine what we think are some of the most insightful and significant aspects of debt being mobilized as a technology of organized differential power. We begin by examining how the imposition of imperial taxation regimes or what we call "imperial monetization" (always backed by force and punishment) contributed to the constitution of new forms of agency geared for the capitalist world market. Unlike Graeber and Braudel, we do not see the market as something separate from capitalism but the very *precondition* for the emergence of capitalization and debt as a technology of organized power. As numeric computational power processes, capitalization and debt can only work through price, and where contracts, transactions, and practices cannot be priced, bought, and sold, the capitalization of debt as technology of power breaks down immediately. Put another way, the market is not space outside of capitalization or debt but the chief enabling mechanism for the accumulation of differential power represented in money (Nitzan and Bichler 2009: 306). We then move on to examine how "national" debts were created and administered in the colonies by focusing on the nascent United States of America and Haiti. We then turn to explore the impact decolonization movements in

Africa and Asia had on these historical structures and the major events leading up to the debt crisis of the 1980s in what today is referred to as the Global South. We conclude the chapter with a brief examination of the sovereign debt crisis in the so-called heartland of global capitalism.

Imperial monetization, transformation, and resistance

European colonial encounters during the so-called age of exploration revealed modes of life, cultural practices, and systems of meaning that were different from those experienced in Christian Europe. Outside Europe, different forms of money and exchange were observed, but in many instances, gold and silver—the main monetary sources coveted by the Europeans—were more likely to be used in decoration for status than as a medium of exchange to be accumulated or invested. In a way, this fact demonstrated that the European fascination with gold and silver as the only "real" money was little more than a socially constructed fetish—albeit, an extremely powerful one. In other words, preconquest populations had established methods and rituals of social reproduction not premised upon capitalist markets and the accumulation of (metallic) money as an end in itself. It is hardly surprising, then, that the colonized were not keen to abandon their generational traditions of social reproduction in order to meet the demands of imperialists for labor, gold and silver, and other goods that could be commodified. As such, one of the key problems faced by the Europeans in achieving differential accumulation in the colonies was native resistance to imperial policies. To be sure, as Rodney (1972: 165) points out in the case of Africa, many West Africans on the coast willingly participated in the colonial money economy introduced by the Europeans, with the transatlantic slave trade being the most obvious example of local involvement (see also Blackburn 2010). However, while some reaped benefits by participating in the growing world market for human energy (slavery) and goods, the vast majority preferred to continue with their own practices of social reproduction outside of capitalist markets. The evidence is more than decisive on the matter given the persistent resistance to colonial policy experienced virtually everywhere Europeans sought to impose their will and the series of punishments and disciplines that were inflicted on recalcitrant social forces that refused to comply with the transformative practices initiated by colonial administrators and businessmen (Stavrianos 1981: 282, 367ff; Miller et al. 1995; Brown 2014). Capitalist markets do not spring up spontaneously, as Marx (1887) and Polanyi ([1944] 1957) rightly recognized and Graeber (2011) confirmed in his recent study. Capitalist markets were socially constructed by the powerful in the quest for differential power and accumulation in an increasingly monetized world order of near constant warfare.

Outside the direct application of violence—including genocidal practices—one of the chief ways traditional forms of social reproduction were transformed, and in many instances destroyed, was through the imposition of imperial taxation regimes. As some early political economists understood—and Marx later emphasized and criticized—taxation was not only the most effective method (outside of direct violence) for enforcing wage-labor but also an efficient technology of expropriation—that is, a mechanism for transferring ownership from direct producers and concentrating it in the hands of capitalists (1887: 530). This time-worn technology of power, applied in the European heartland to fund "national" debts amassed to finance dynastic wars and fund the savagery of for-profit colonial projects, would be imposed anew in the colonies. The evidence of taxation being used as an imposed debt obligation with transformative effects is best illustrated by the case of colonial Africa, where it was applied near ubiquitously regardless of the colonizer (Rodney 1972; Stavrianos 1981: 300ff; Wray 1998: 57ff; Bush and Maltby 2004; Forstater 2005). Let us consider some examples in the context of colonial enterprise.

As suggested above, one of the fundamental problems faced by colonialists was how to obtain the necessary labor to make their newly acquired lands or mines profitable. Appropriating land through violence and fraud was one thing, recruiting a labor force loyal to colonial projects, quite another altogether. Even when the local communities were promised wages for work, they more often than not declined the offer. The natives had little need for wages when they could reproduce their own livelihoods outside of the colonial market. One of the main ways this imperial "problem" was overcome was for colonial administrators to impose a cattle, hut, or head (poll) tax on the local population that *had to be paid in the currency issued by the colonizer.* Since failure to pay the required tax was met with strict punishment, those who complied found themselves converting part of their land into cash crops (e.g., cotton, groundnuts, flowers) that could be sold for the imperial currency needed to settle their tax debt to the sovereign authorities. Forstater (2005: 60–61), Marks (in Oliver and Sanderson 1985: 456), Killingray (1986),[1] and others have documented punishments including: the burning of huts, shooting, the seizure of cattle and goods, fines, prison labor, and public shaming. For example, tax debtors in Burkina Faso who refused payment were forced to chant the prayer *Puennam co mam ligidi* or translated— "God, give me money"—throughout the day under the scathing heat of the tropical sun. Others would be forced to run around the administrative building while carrying their wife, or—in the case of polygamous relationships—wives, on their backs. Wives would then have to take a turn piggy-backing their husband around the building. Where growing cash crops proved more difficult, Africans had to turn to wage-labor in order to satisfy their need for colonial currency. With the prospect of inevitable crop failures from time to time as well as the arbitrary nature of taxation, many struggled to pay their taxes in relatively scarce colonial currency. In order to avoid punishment, many Africans resorted to local moneylenders who were often more than happy to extend usurious loans to producers in return for collateral (land) they often assumed when debts could not be repaid. Tax debt was a forcing house for the concentration of property in fewer hands just as much as it was the motive force compelling Africans to work for their colonial masters. Indeed, perpetual tax debt on top of credit taken from moneylenders created a permanent force of wage-laborers since taxation made money a necessity to avoid punitive measures.

The final way in which tax debt operated as a technology of power was through the corvée system. Instead of imposing a tax to be paid in colonial money, a certain amount of labor was demanded by locals to discharge the tax. In many instances this was a preferred practice of labor recruitment since it could even operate in an environment where money was scarce (Oliver and Sanderson 1985: 527). The tax was paid back in hours and days worked for others rather than one's own family or the community and the work often involved considerable migration. But whichever way debt was mobilized in its specificity as a technology of power, one thing is certain: its operation had transformative effects on social relations and served the colonists by severing the colonized from their previous patterns of social reproduction. What is more, an uneven regime of economic growth and environmental transformation was being increasingly thrust upon local communities through imperial monetization brought on by taxation. In our theorization of debt as a technology of organized power, the concept of "imperial monetization" means at least two things. First, the term captures the process whereby imperial or colonial powers impose their monetary system upon a society that coordinated their economic interdependence and social reproduction in some other fashion. Over time, this meant the juridical sabotage or banning of alternative forms of currency used by Africans such as the Maria Theresa thaler (dollar), manillas, and cowries (Ofonagoro 1979; Ubah 1980; Uche 1999; Mwangi 2001; Helleiner 2002a; Hermann 2011).[2] For colonial policy to be effective, imperial money was to be made exclusive and the practice of accounting a weapon (Annisette and Neu 2004). Second, imperial monetization also refers to the process whereby debts are contracted in an imperial or colonial currency. This second role accomplishes two goals: first, it helps expand the imperial money supply through the extension of new loans to foreigners to pay for capital imports from Europe. These loans effectively capitalized the exploitive capacity of the colonies and their ability to repay debt to creditors (e.g., cash crops, mines, infrastructural projects, and later fossil fuels). Engels noticed this relationship in a supplement to volume three of Marx's *Capital*:

Then colonisation. Today this is purely a subsidiary of the stock exchange, in whose interests the European powers divided Africa a few years ago, and the French conquered Tunis and Tonkin. Africa leased directly to companies (Niger, South Africa, German South-West and German East Africa), and Mashonaland and Natal seized by Rhodes for the stock exchange. (quoted in Marx 1981: 1047)

What this passage suggests is that the riches of the colonies and the radical changes in social relations imposed on indigenous forces were effectively being capitalized by investors in the stock markets of Europe. Second, the extension of these loans often resulted in the creation of unrepayable "national" debts owed to foreign interests in the foreign currency borrowed. We will discuss this role and its implications in greater detail in the last two sections of this chapter.

Yet imperial monetization was not without its contradictions and we should be mindful not to theorize it as a universal law being applied as a linear and unwavering strategy despite its eventual ubiquity before national independence movements. For example, many European traders preferred to continue the practice of barter trade with local traders. There appears to be two primary reasons why this was so. First, barter established personal relationships between traders, and the Europeans could take advantage of price differentials in goods—often dictated by themselves and an early form of unequal exchange. Second, it was thought that if African traders entered the monetized world they would out-compete and potentially out-accumulate their European counterparts (Hermann 2011). In other words, continuing to use barter as a principal form of trade was one way for individual firms to sabotage local competing interests. However, colonial administrators understood that these private forms of barter were not helpful in advancing a uniform and exclusive standard of colonial money, and where possible, they challenged rogue traders.

It is of course true, to some extent, as more sympathetic scholars of imperialism are wont to emphasize, that taxes were often used to finance public works of one kind or another. For example, infrastructure projects such as the setting up of railroads, hospitals, ports, and dykes were said to benefit local populations despite the fact that they largely benefited private capitalists. In this view, colonial taxation was largely a collective project of mutual benefit in the agelong quest to better standards of living and to "civilize" the natives through Western commercial growth and modes of life. But as more critical scholars have pointed out, whatever biopolitics were at play—that is to say, at least in this context, whatever attempts to improve life by directing infrastructural projects—they were likely ancillary to the primary drive of imposing new forms of capitalist social reproduction on populations increasingly policed by an apparatus of imperial discipline, punishment, and surveillance (Wray 1998: 60). We should recall, as Rodney reminds us, that debt-funded "public works" also included "building castles for governors, prisons for Africans, barracks for troops, and bungalows for colonial officials" (1972: 166).

The imposition of debt-taxes on colonial populations in Africa is illustrative of the Chartalist or state theory of money that argues, following the original formulation of Knapp, that a sovereign or ruler pays for its goods and services in a definite form of money, which is accepted by the providers of those goods and services because this particular form of money is needed to service the imposed or imputed taxes (Wray 2002, 2004). Wray summarized what this process entailed for more orthodox accounts of money's origins:

> the case of the colonial governors may be a more powerful test of the taxes-drive-money thesis than is readily apparent, for here is a case in which taxes are imposed by an external authority whose only legitimacy in the eyes of the population might be threat of use of force… However, the power to tax and to define the form in which the tax would be paid set in motion the process of monetization of the economy. The important point is that "monetization" did not spring forth from barter; nor did it require "trust"—as most stories about the origins of money claim. (1998: 61)

In other words, the monetization and transformation of African social reproduction was no spontaneous affair stemming from the natural propensity of Africans to "truck, barter and trade" with their imperial masters, but a direct colonial imposition backed by force. It was not long before "taxation heightened popular aggravation and figured prominently in movements of protest and rebellion" (Wright in Oliver and Sanderson 1985: 590). Of the numerous examples of tax rebellions, revolts, and riots to draw on as illustrations from in the colonies, we only outline two in summary below (for a compendium see Burg 2004).

The Deccan riots

Long before the twenty-first-century epidemic of peasant suicides in rural India, the practice of lending money to peasant cultivators by a small class of creditors pervaded the village community. As a caste, however, their power had been limited by the way in which social power was divided in rural society. Until 1828, when the British colonial administration started to administer market reforms in Maharashtra, moneylenders—or *vanis*—extended money to a village community in the hope of making a return on their capital. Crucially, these loans were not collateralized, allowing for a historically unique (and perhaps strange) cooperation between moneylenders and cultivators. The constitution of this interdependence rested in the fact that the power of the *vanis* was restricted in at least two important ways. First, before colonial rule, *vanis* could not expropriate peasant land to repay debts because land was held by the village and could not be alienated. Second, as Metcalf remarked, "the state, on its part, gave the moneylender no assistance in the recovery of debts. If not actively hostile, it was apathetic, and left the creditor to collect his due as best he could" (1962: 390; see also Kumar 2011: 614). With the onset of more market-oriented governance from 1828, these relations of force would be realigned by three colonial innovations that unleashed debt as a technology of power on village cultivators. First, the British performed surveys on the land and accorded private property titles to individual cultivators rather than to the village as a whole. This act not only individualized property ownership but also valued or "priced" the land held by farmers. Second, a colonial legal apparatus was erected to enforce private property rights. Third, believing their two previous initiatives would spur greater agricultural productivity, successive colonial administrators applied ever-heavier direct taxation on the cultivators. While rural farmers did borrow money in times of crop failure or to pay for marriages, feasts, and social ceremonies, Metcalf (1962) has argued that the overwhelming reason cultivators borrowed from the *vanis* was because of the debt they owed in taxes to the colonial administration.[3] Now, when the *vanis* extended credit under British rule, they demanded that cultivators advance their land as collateral. As debts mounted due to usurious interest rates, poor harvests, declining terms of trade, mounting taxes, or some combination thereof, the *vanis* used the court system to enforce their contracts with debtors. As a consequence, more and more cultivators lost possession of their land. Kumar noted what these agrarian changes meant "the dispossessed peasant was forced to live as a landless laborer, often on those very fields which he had formerly cultivated as an independent proprietor" (2011: 619). What made matters even more unjust was the fact that the entirety of the land was often seized when only a few payments were in arrears. Increasingly, land was being concentrated in the hands of the wealthier few as happened elsewhere where mass indebtedness pervaded rural society.[4] By 1875, dispossession, indebtedness, and burdensome taxes were so widespread throughout the Deccan that cultivators directed their anger at the *vanis* and rioted. As Kumar argued, the object of these riots was "to obtain and destroy the bonds and decrees possessed by the moneylenders" in order to destroy them (2011: 634). As long as the moneylender gave up his debt-obligations and accounting records peacefully, little harm was done to his person or property. Where records were not given up so easily, violence typically ensued. Over time, the riots subsided but widespread indebtedness remained. Fearing another revolt, colonial administrators eventually put in place measures to protect cultivators from moneylenders, though these actions came after fifty years of British rule and unmistakable transformations in previous forms of rural social reproduction and power relations.

The Bambatha Rebellion

Another key moment in the resistance to colonial taxation is the Bambatha Rebellion, an armed revolt in the Natal region of South Africa personalized by the name of its minor Zulu leader. A colonial hut tax had already been imposed on married African men in Natal but it was often their sons who migrated to the cities or mines to earn money to pay the tax (Redding 2000: 38). By 1887, the previously independent political state of Zululand had been militarily defeated and came under the control of British colonial administrators. Much of the available arable land in the region was confiscated by white settlers and the hut tax was imposed on Zulu men. Defeat in battle was made worse by a series of natural calamities that killed cattle and ruined crops. In this dire situation, many were drawn to the gold and diamond mines, where they could earn better wages with which to pay or contribute to the hut tax of their father. But this posed a problem for white agricultural settlers who wanted to recruit African labor for their farms. Under pressure from white settlers, colonial officials introduced a £1 poll tax on all African men above eighteen years of age—an application of power facilitated by a census that had been taken of the region in 1905. While some were ambivalent about the new tax, others viewed the levy as accelerating and compounding changes in precolonial social relations. Once again, previous forms of social reproduction were being disturbed at the household level by a debt-tax—what Tilly called the "invasions of small-scale social life" (1990: 25). By 1906, Bambatha along with other Zulu chiefs and tribesmen refused to pay the new tax and after a skirmish with authorities that led to the death of two colonial officers, martial law was declared by the colonial administration in Natal. After some minor attacks against colonial forces, Bambatha and his forces were held up in Mome Gorge, where they were eventually hunted like dogs and gunned down by the thousands (Zulus spears and shields being largely ineffective against steel and gunpowder). As Pakenham put it, "the Zulus learnt a bitter lesson about the realities of power" that day (1992: 649). Arguably, the lesson they learned was that British rule and debt in the form of a poll tax was backed by the power of heavy artillery and machine guns. While records vary, it is estimated that 3,000–4,000 Zulus were killed, 5,000–7,000 imprisoned, and 4,000 or so flogged by colonial authorities. Huts were also razed to the ground throughout the conflict (Marks 1970; Stuart 1913; Pakenham 1992: 649; Redding 2000). The rebellion's leader, Bambatha, was eventually captured, killed, and decapitated. When the governor of Natal sought to commemorate the victory with a medal in the honor of the dozen or so white men who had fallen, none other than Winston Churchill replied that it would be better to strike a new copper coin with Bambatha's head on it as a more appropriate symbol of the colonizer's sacrifice in blood. Imperial monetization not only encountered resistance but proposed to strike its victims upon its coins!

The birth of the "national" debt in the colonies

As in the case of imperial monetization through enforceable tax debt, we do not have the space to examine the proliferation and amplification of "national" debts. Demonstrating the near ubiquity of the phenomenon, there are currently only four countries in the world *without* national debts: Brunei, Liechtenstein, Palau, and Niue. The reader can be forgiven if they are unfamiliar with these countries since they are largely negligible to the global economy, where sovereign debt now stands at $58 trillion and mounting by the second.[5] The United States of America and Japan make up just under half of all sovereign debt ($25 trillion). But while we cannot offer a full historical account of the development of "national" debts here, we investigate the creation of "national" debts in: (1) colonial America before and after its revolutionary war with imperial Britain, and (2) the indemnity largely forced on a newly independent republic of Haiti founded by a successful slave revolution. As we shall see, and as addressed in Chapter 2, a key facet of instituting a "national" debt is not only that it was initially capitalized by a small coterie of private social forces but also that it was meant to be permanent. Without this institutional permanence, debt could not act as a technology of organized power mobilized by the few for their own private accumulation. At the liberal end of the critiques of imperialism, Hobson captured the essence of debt being mobilized as a technology power inside and outside Europe:

> The creation of public debts is a normal and a most imposing feature of Imperialism... It is a *direct object of imperialist finance to create further debts*, just as it is an object of the private money-lender to goad his clients into pecuniary difficulties in order that they may have recourse to him. Analysis of foreign investments shows that public or State-guaranteed debts are largely held by investors and financiers of other nations; and recent history shows, in the cases of Egypt, Turkey, China, the hand of the bond-holder, and of the potential bond-holder, in politics. This method of finance is not only profitable in the case of foreign nations, where it is a chief instrument or pretext for encroachment. *It is of service to the financial classes to have a large national debt of their own.* The floating of and the dealing in such public loans are a profitable business, and are means of exercising important political influences at critical junctures. (Hobson 2005: 108, emphasis added)

In other words, the national debt as a technology of power has an internal and external dimension. Internal insofar as it was used as a weapon against subordinate social forces to limit certain political possibilities. The modern corollary is clear enough: in the age of so-called neoliberal austerity, the national debt is used to justify the reconfiguration of power relations between state and society through privatizations, cutbacks in social spending (wages, infrastructure, pensions), and increases in tax and public service provisions (user fees). In its external or international dimension, the financiers of creditor nations can essentially reconfigure the established patterns of social reproduction of indebted countries when they fail to service debts and have insufficient power to defend their national sovereignty. We will discuss this below but it is largely accomplished by advisors and "experts" effectively commandeering the fiscal and monetary policy of the state to ensure debt repayment. There is little doubt that domestic elites are often complicit in the project. The United States of America reflected both these dimensions before and after its revolutionary war against Imperial Britain.

The birth of the United States national debt

The British colonization of North America was a profit-seeking endeavor sponsored by the Crown but largely financed by private initiative. Indeed, Richard Hakluyt's *Discourse Concerning Western Planting* (1584) can be read as one of the first "company prospectuses" aimed at convincing the Crown and investors of the benefits of Western colonization (Micklethwait and Wooldrige 2003: 18–19). How convincing this tract was is unclear, but a Western colonial project was soon sanctioned and proceeded in one of two ways. First, wealthy individuals (mainly around London) interested in the accumulation of money formed joint-stock trading companies and petitioned the Crown for an exclusive charter to certain tracts of North American land and trade. These "grants of land made by England served as centers of monopoly power to the companies" (Curtis 2014: 481). What this means is that the colonial enterprise was a capitalized project with the capitalization of colonial firms largely contingent on their monopoly privileges and their ability to make profit for their investors. This involved removing, killing, and swindling the native population out of their ancestral lands, and as we will see, debt was mobilized as an effective technology of power here too. The second way North America was colonized was by proprietorship. This was simply the act of the Crown granting land to individuals or a small band of individuals as either a favor or to resolve royal debts. For example, King Charles II granted what we today call Pennsylvania and Delaware to William Penn in return for cancelling a £16,000 debt that was owed to his father (Curtis 2014: 484). Debt and capitalization, then, were motive forces for English colonialism. They would also play an integral role in the founding of a new nation free of imperial control and its national debt.

Before the American War of Independence (1775–83) and the coming into force of the Constitution of the United States (1789), there were two inescapable facts of colonial life among the settlers: the ubiquity of debt at all levels of society and the scarcity of money for trade and the settlement of debt. Mann captured the daily reality of indebtedness: "debt cut across regional, class, and occupational lines. Whether one was an Atlantic merchant or a rural shopkeeper, a tidewater planter or a backwoods farmer, debt was an integral part of daily life" (2003: 3). There were of course different types of debt found in the thirteen colonies and five main sources of currency for which debt could be incurred or settled: (1) furs and wampum; (2) commodity money or "Country Money" such as tobacco, indigo, wheat, and maize; (3) foreign coins, particularly of Spanish and Portuguese origin; (4) British coinage; and (5) various types of paper money or colonial scrip (Davies 2002: 459). Depending on the transaction, these mediums of exchange were all potentially useful. However, the scarcity of money problem largely resulted from the fact that gold and silver (as in Europe and elsewhere) were treated as the only "real" money. Since there were no domestic mines of gold and silver discovered early on in British North America, colonists had to rely on trade in order to attract coined money or bills of exchange redeemable for sterling (Ferguson 1954: 158; Davies 2002: 458). However, since the colonies were heavily dependent on imports from Britain for conveniences and luxuries, they suffered chronic shortages of currency since more money was being paid to British merchants than was earned abroad by selling domestic cash crops like tobacco.[6] Moreover, money was required for domestic transactions and internal development, and there was not enough specie to facilitate the potential capacity of domestic trade. With a dearth of specie, the colonists turned to paper currency as a primary medium of exchange. There were two ways in which paper money could be issued: (1) colonial legislatures could print and spend the paper currency into the economy, mainly to finance the expense of war, and/or (2) they could set up a loan office or land bank to lend to farmers at low interest based on the security of the farmer's land

(Ferguson 1954: 168). By most accounts, these paper notes eased internal and some external transactions and spurred what we would today call economic growth. It could also be used to pay taxes and, in places, purchase land. For most intents and purposes, the colonial scrip issued by the thirteen legislatures was considered legal tender or acceptable to meet financial obligations.

At first, London tolerated the paper currency since there was a recognized dearth of gold and silver in the colonies to facilitate trade. However, by 1751 the Parliament was pressured by creditors and mercantile interests to pass an act restricting paper money. Specifically, these interests wanted to ban legal tender laws that would allow settlers to settle their debts in colonial scrip (Ferguson 1954: 177). The act did just that but only applied to New England, where creditors were worried about being paid in depreciated currency. By the time the French and Indian War was terminated in favor of imperial Britain (1754–63), more paper currency south of New England had been emitted. The scrip was issued to help pay for the prolonged conflict, but now that peace had resumed, merchants and creditors feared that they would be forced to accept depreciated paper for sterling debts (Greene and Jellison 1961: 486; Sosin 1964: 175). Their concerns were heard, and in 1764, another currency act was passed banning legal tender laws in the remaining provinces. Elite colonists protested against the currency acts but British officials would not repeal the legislation. This forced the provinces to seek a number of compromises, some of which were successful in resolving the scarcity of money problem. Still, without legal tender laws, debts to British creditors and merchants now had to be paid in sterling unless otherwise agreed. This caused considerable financial difficulties in New Jersey, Virginia, the Carolinas, and Georgia in the decade before the American Revolutionary War. To be sure, at the First Continental Congress (1774), the Currency Act of 1764 was listed as one of the many violations of colonial rights (Greene and Jellison 1961: 518). While the currency issue may not have been a leading impetus for taking up arms against Britain, Greene and Jellison (1961) have convincingly argued that it was certainly a major grievance. As we will argue below, the other major grievances were also largely connected to debt and the desire for pecuniary accumulation among colonial elites.

The historiography of the American Revolution and the subsequent political settlement are vast. However, up until the work of Charles Beard (1913), most scholarly accounts were celebratory or, in Curtis' words, "chauvinistic" (2014: 475). In these renditions, the founding fathers were heralded as political geniuses who compromised to achieve a more perfect union than the Articles of Confederation allowed (for a critical reading of the events leading up to the Constitution, see Di Muzio in Gill and Cutler 2014: 81–94). To do so they had to overcome the antifederalists who were skeptical about protecting the interest of citizens and their liberties within a large rather than a small territorial unit.[7] Building on the politico-economic observations Madison scribed in *Federalist 10*, Beard's thesis argued that the constitutional settlement was primarily a work of men with financial vested interests trying to protect their property *vis-à-vis* their lesser counterparts (1913: 31–51). A constitution that authorized a national government would not only be able to secure unequal property in the present but also provide the organized force (rather than the disparate force of the Continental Congress under the Articles of Confederation) required to open up further avenues for the accumulation of wealth west of the Appalachians. At first, the most damaging charges launched against Beard's thesis was that it was overly deterministic (that is, to say it was derived from economic interests solely), and the founders did not always seem to vote in their immediate economic interests. Current historians share some of this critique but argue that given the political-economy of the time and the goal of the federalists, Beard was correct to focus on the financial or economic interests of those arguing for a new "national" government (Holton 1999; 2004; 2005b; Curtis 2014). Given the discourse of the antifederalists and the popular social forces that were politicized during the revolution, things certainly could have been otherwise. But they were not. As one of the most prominent historians of the period argued, the federal Constitution was designed not only to "transfer power from the many to the few" but to secure unequal property, power, and privilege well into the future (Wood 1969: 516 citing Richard Henry Lee; see also Nedelsky 1990: 2). But the ratification of the Constitution was not the only strategic move made by federalists. Under Hamilton's initiatives, the new political settlement was to be backed up by a national debt and a for-profit, government-sponsored "national" bank. To understand why, we have to consider the situation leaders of the revolution found themselves in and what they wished to accomplish with the creation of an independent, centralized government.

The first major grievance of colonial elites, many of whom were deeply in debt to British creditors and merchants for their lifestyle, was the Royal Proclamation of 1763 and the Quebec Act of 1774 (Morris 1962: 15; Curtis 2014: 456–457). The Proclamation of 1763 was "a royal decree forbidding settlement or the purchase of Indian lands west of a line drawn along the crest of the Appalachians" (Ferguson 1979: 32). The primary reason for the decree was the considerable debt Britain had incurred fighting the French and Indian War from 1754 to 1763 (part of the broader Seven's Years War internationally). London thought that if colonists continued to press westward by usurping or purchasing Indian lands, this would provoke further wars with the Indians and thus produce even more debt. They also wanted to protect Indian hunting grounds from settlement since British merchants had a lucrative business trading with the Indians of the interior.[8] "In effect, the Proclamation denied wealthy merchants, landowners and their companies access to vast tracts of land that could have been resold to settlers or used in the production of cash crops" like tobacco (Holton 1999: 3ff; Di Muzio 2014: 88). Since land was the primary source of wealth before the fossil fuel revolution, the decree placed a strict limit on the further accumulation of money and economic growth by exploiting western land inhabited by native tribes. The Quebec Act and additional land reform measures, which followed over a decade later, only compounded these problems by granting the Ohio Country to the province of Quebec, thereby nullifying land claims made by the thirteen colonies to the region. What made matters worse was not only the fact that native land was to be commodified and was viewed as a *future* profit-making enterprise but also the fact that the ownership and sale of new lands was virtually the only way in which politically connected plantation owners could repay their mounting debts to British merchants.[9] Indeed, by 1766, a parliamentary committee found that about £4.5 million was due to British merchants in America with nine-tenths of the debt accounted for by Southern planters (Sosin 1964: 175 nt. 4; Friedenberg 1992: 149; Holton 1999: 35–36; cf. Evans 1962). Breen records why these new acts would have disturbed Southern planters so:

> … the great planters … used their positions on the governor's council or in the House of Burgesses to patent huge tracts of western lands .… The great planters held on to some choice pieces of property… but most of it was resold … at considerable profit .… This cozy system lasted until the early 1750s when the French and Indian War, coupled with tighter imperial controls over the granting of western lands, cut the gentry off from one of its major sources of income. (Breen 1985: 35–36)

According to Holton (1999), Bouton (2001), and Curtis (2014), the pressure of debt and the loss of the ability to appropriate, improve, or sell indigenous land in the west were enough to motivate key figures like Washington, Jefferson, Mason, and Lee to play key leadership roles in the armed struggle against imperial Britain.

But if debt was mobilized as a technology of power by British merchants against their colonial brethren, it was reapplied by the North American aristocracy of landowners and merchants to Native American tribes. Indeed, outside direct violence, one of the main ways that Indian communities lost their land was by going into debt to merchant settlers or colonial governments. If and when they could not repay these debts (and they typically could not, as more and more of their hunting grounds were being depleted of resources), then land was appropriated by creditors or colonial officials. In a private letter to William Henry Harrison, who was to negotiate treaties with Indians under Jefferson, the new president was candid about Indian policy under his administration:

> To promote this disposition to ex-change lands, which they [native Indians] have to spare and we want, for necessaries, which we have

to spare and they want, we shall push our trading uses, and be glad to see the good and influential individuals among them run in debt, because we observe that when these debts get beyond what the individuals can pay, they become willing to lop them off by a cession of lands... In this way our settlements will gradually circumscribe and approach the Indians, and they will in time either incorporate with us as citizens of the United States, or remove beyond the Mississippi. The former is certainly the termination of their history most happy for themselves; but, in the whole course of this, it is essential to cultivate their love. As to their fear, we presume that our strength and their weakness is now so visible that they must see we have only to shut our hand to crush them ... Should any tribe be fool-hardy enough to take up the hatchet at any time, the seizing the whole country of that tribe, and driving them across the Mississippi, as the only condition of peace, would be an example to others, and a furtherance of our final consolidation.[10]

This could not be a clearer statement of how debt is to be mobilized as a weapon of the powerful in order to expropriate the native population from their ancestral lands. The impetus to do this was made significantly more acute after the American Revolutionary War and the constitutional settlement because the new government itself was in considerable debt to wealthy patriots and foreign creditors. As Banner notes, this relationship was well understood by the Continental Congress before a federal government was introduced:

Federal and state governments also had large money debts. In the short run they needed assets that could be sold to pay creditors. In the longer run, if they hoped to be able to borrow in the future, they would need a conspicuous stream of income to entice creditors to lend. The most obvious source of money in both the present and the future was the sale of public land. "The public creditors have been led to believe and have a right to expect," the Continental Congress concluded, "that those territories will be speedily improved into a fund towards the security and payment of the national debt." But the government had to acquire land before it could sell land, and the only people from whom land could be acquired were the Indians. (2005: 127)

With imperial Britain defeated, the new federal government was free to pass its own legislation opening up the western frontier for further land speculation and settlement. These initiatives, as the quote suggests, were intimately tied to the creation of a national debt that used western lands as a security (Williams 1966: 134). Still, private social forces also leveraged the power of the national debt to assist in their acquisition of profit. For example, in the 1790s, Panton, Leslie and Co. began purchasing and consolidating the small and diffuse debts of southern tribes. Once they had a pool of debt (undoubtedly discounted from their original issuers), the firm used their power to petition the national government for a deal. According to Banner, by 1805 their efforts were successful. The federal government paid the Indian debt capitalized by the company and in return added about 8 million acres of indigenous land to the national coffers (2005: 126).[11] Something very similar also happened with the outstanding debts incurred by the state and union governments in financing their war with imperial London.

With a dearth of specie, the only way in which the American Revolutionary War could be financed was through the issuance of paper money, most of which was issued as debt of some kind by state legislatures or the union government. After the war (1783), the fiscal situations of the victorious provinces were in disarray and a severe depression resulted from a lack of specie and the scarcity of money and credit. Desperate for hard money to pay taxes and to settle debts that were often incurred to support families while in battle, many farmers and other middling settlers were forced to sell their land. Being forced to sell land to meet tax and additional debt payments ignited one of the most infamous resistance movements in postrevolutionary America: Shay's Rebellion (1786–7). The goal of the 2,000-strong farmer rebellion was to shut down courthouses that were responsible for hearing the pleas of creditors and sanctioning the sale of land for debt and tax payments.[12]

Since a number of state militia were supportive of the movement, wealthy property owners of Massachusetts were forced to finance their own private army to suppress the revolt (Smith 1948; Szatmary 1980; Brown 1983).

Yet another way in which desperate settlers aimed to get by was by selling army certificates they had received in payment for military service to the revolutionary governments. Desperate for money to pay taxes or afford their livelihood in a period of economic depression, many soldiers and widows sold their certificates to wealthy speculators at what was often an extreme discount. While the debates are not definitive, there is considerable evidence to suggest that what made matters worse was the knowledge that an organized force of propertied interests were going to vie for a national government with the power to tax in order to meet the revolutionary debt and hold democracy at the state level in check because of debtor relief programs and the desire to overcome the scarcity of currency through the issuance of paper money (Ferguson 1954; Bogin 1989; Mann 2003: 176; Holton 2004; Wright 2008). While some of the war debt was capitalized to weaken the British Empire by enemies from France, Spain, and the United Provinces, the overwhelming majority of debt issues from the revolutionary period were owned by domestic social forces (Davies 2002: 467). How widespread revolutionary debts were held by the end of the war is a matter of considerable dispute; and given that a series of fires in the treasury destroyed federal records, it is unlikely that we will ever get definitive proof of the original distribution of ownership (Ferguson 1954: 35).[13] However, there is strong evidence to suggest that most of the debt repayments did not go to the initial holders of the debt but to a small number of speculators who concentrated government securities in their own hands by buying up claims at considerable discounts. This was done in the anticipation that a central government with the power to tax would eventually come to fruition and pay back the debt at face value (Ferguson 1954; Mann 2003: 176; Wright 2008: 124). There is little doubt that one of the chief concerns of the men who met at the Philadelphia Convention was how to finance the debt accumulated during the war (Wright 2008: 81). Suspicious of distant and centralized power, the Articles of Confederation purposely created a weak federated government without the power to tax—one of the chief reasons why Continental dollars depreciated in value throughout the war (Wray 1998: 62; Loubert 2012: 448–449). Although they only had a mandate to suggest needed changes to the Articles of Confederation, those present at the conference embarked upon creating a strong national constitution that would take the power of money creation and debt relief out of the hands of state legislatures. These legislatures had often proved too democratic and sympathetic to the needs of their constituents, and where they were not, protests typically ensued creating instability and disrespect for "property" (Wood 1969; Edling and Kaplanoff 2004; Holton 2005a). To be sure, addressing the national debt problem and curtailing the rights of states were not the only goals of the framers. But here we are concentrating on the effects of the Constitution as it pertains to debt as a technology of power, and the constitutional settlement and its institutional development accomplished some very important goals in the service of the powerful. When thinking about the initiatives we list below, the reader would do well to recall the progressive thesis that there were really two American revolutions: the first, a popular struggle of diverse social forces that fought against imperial Britain, and the second, counter-revolution by colonial elites who wanted to stem the radicalism and democratic spirit of the revolution once victory was claimed for the former colonies (for an overview of this historiographical tradition, see Morris 1962: 20ff; Wood 1969: 483ff; Fresia 1988; Tise 1998). While the elite counter-revolutionary program was never without contestation, the propertied men of the Philadelphia Convention achieved considerable success in creating the foundations of an empire premised upon unequal property and slavery with a national debt and privately capitalized "public" bank at its center.

The important constitutional initiatives that locked in debt as an organized technology of power were as follows. Article 1, Section 8 gave power to the Congress to "lay and collect taxes, duties, imposts and excises"—a power never granted to the Continental Congress by the state governments. With the power to tax, the Congress could now officially enforce the collection of money to repay rich creditors of the revolutionary war debt and future debt incurred by war. As

Brown (1989: 1) detailed, up until the Great Depression most of the debt contracted by the US government was due to war or the preparation for war. Article 1, Section 10 effectively removed the power of state legislatures to create money and forced states to accept gold and silver as the only legal tender for debts. Since Americans were fonder of their local and state legislatures because they were more proximate centers of democratic power, this was a massive blow to democracy and led toward the centralization of monetary power. Section VI of the Constitution could not have been a clearer gift to the speculators who had busied themselves purchasing US debt paper at deep discounts from desperate farmers and soldiers. It stated that "all debts contracted and engagements entered into, before the adoption of this constitution, shall be as valid against the United States under this constitution." The technical details of financing what would become a consolidated "national" debt were not worked out by Secretary of the Treasury Alexander Hamilton until 1790. Hamilton's first initiative was to boost the creditworthiness of the new government by announcing that all debts issued by the Continental Congress would be honored to present, rather than original, holders. This, no doubt, delighted speculators and increased the value of their securities. Hamilton's second initiative was to assume all state debts and aggregate them under one federally funded "national" debt. This move helped to pacify state resistance to the centralization of financial power by unburdening them of the responsibility to impose unpopular taxes. By 1804, even private debts of wealthy colonists were absorbed under the "national" debt, a trick, as we shall see in the following section, played by international bankers during the so-called Third World Debt Crisis of the 1970s and 1980s (Henry 2003; Curtis 2014: 456). Third, to raise revenue to service interest on the national debt, Hamilton introduced taxes on imports and particularly wine, spirits, tea, and coffee. This tax was regressive since it shifted the burden of taxation away from income and property and applied to the rich and poor alike. But while this new tax helped to finance the burgeoning national debt, most speculators understood that the real prize held by the federal government was the ability to appropriate and dispense native lands to favorites. If the power of the federal government was capitalized through its national debt, it was the power of the government to enforce the destruction of native forms of social reproduction and capture their land. Two further initiatives are worth mentioning. In 1792, the Coinage Act was passed, making the American silver dollar the official money of account in the United States and juridically (though not in practice until much later) banning all other forms of foreign money from interior circulation. Finally, Hamilton thought to erect a national bank on the model of the Bank of England to hold Treasury deposits and service the interest on government debt (Sylla 1998; Cowen 2000; Konings 2011: 28). Although there were slight differences with the Bank of England (Wright 2008: 155), the first Bank of the United States (BUS) was a for-profit, capitalized chartered bank owned by a majority of private shareholders (Rothbard 2002: 68ff). The BUS was capitalized at $10 million, with the federal government paying in $2 million and outside investors the remainder. Investors could also use their outstanding government bonds to purchase shares in the new bank. Thus the national debt was born of war and the power of private creditors. Over the coming centuries, through continental expansion into native and Mexican territory and extracontinental wars powered by fossil fuels, the national debt would grow to become the world's largest. When debt is understood as a technology of power, is it any wonder to find that the world's most powerful nation is also its most indebted?

Colonization, decolonization, and national debts

We discussed the creation of a national debt in the United States in some detail not only because it was modeled on the union of state power and private finance as in England but also because it turned out to be one of the most successful at leveraging the power of the state in the pursuit of war, social transformation, and capitalist accumulation. If the level of capitalization is a measure of investor confidence in the ability of any organized corporate force to shape and reshape the terrain of global social reproduction and world politics, then at least since the Second World War, investors have squarely placed their confidence with the US government and its military apparatus to enforce change and maintain world order (Arrighi 1994; Di Muzio 2007).

Unlike the United States, which managed to extricate itself from the imperial grip of Britain, most other states acquired their "national" debts during the process of empire building and, more often than not, under the colonial gun of infrastructural projects for resource extraction. As yet, there is no comprehensive study on the emergence of national debts worldwide, but from our initial research we can make at least two theoretical observations based on historical evidence. First, "national" debts, particularly in the colonies, have their beginnings in the colonial practice of making "colonies pay for their own exploitation and conquest" (Anghie 2005: 172). Typically, this meant that the government would assume large capital investments primarily made by foreign business interests so that resources could be extracted and sold to external markets for private profit (Rodney 1972: 209). Given that this required "structural adjustment" of previous forms of social reproduction, the colonies were often forced to finance their own policing and colonial foreign policy. Nehru discussed this in his study of British rule in India:

> Thus India had to bear the cost of her own conquest, and then of her transfer (or sale) from the East India Company to the British Crown, for the extension of the British Empire to Burma and elsewhere, for expeditions to Africa, Persia, etc., and for her defence against Indians themselves. She was not only used as a base for imperial purposes, without any reimbursement for this, but she had further to pay for the training of part of the British Army in England—"capitation" charges these were called. Indeed India was charged for all manner of other expenses incurred by Britain, such as the maintenance of British diplomatic and consular establishments in China and Persia, the entire cost of the telegraph line from England to India, part of the expenses of the British Mediterranean fleet, and even the

receptions given to the Sultan of Turkey in London. (1946: 305; see also Stavrianos 1981: 124 for additional expenses "incurred" by the colonial government)

These measures and others were financed by heavy taxation on the majority of the population: a peasantry increasingly squeezed and brought to the brink of survival.[14]

Second, if "national" debts did not result from foreign investments and colonial administration charged to the state coffers, they were often enforced upon a population as an indemnity through force of arms. The examples of Haiti and China are perhaps the most prominent. Before Haiti became the first black republic to dot the world map, the country was the imperial possession of France and known as Saint-Domingue (from 1697). Since the native population was decimated by Spain's initial colonial encounter, African slaves were imported to work the coffee and sugar plantations owned by Europeans. A rigid and brutal racial and class structure emerged, but one that did allow some slaves to earn their freedom. By the time the slaves took up arms against their oppressors, Haiti was France's wealthiest colonial possession, producing 60 percent of the world's coffee and 40 percent of its sugar. By 1804, and despite continued European attempts to crush the revolution in its infancy, the slaves won their independence. However, in an Atlantic world replete with slavery, Haiti was politically and economically isolated. To gain international recognition from France, Haitian leaders agreed to pay France reparations for the loss of its property to the tune of 150 million francs in gold. This was an incredible sum to pay and to do so Haiti had to take "out huge loans from American, German and French banks, at exorbitant rates of interest. By 1900, Haiti was spending about 80% of its national budget on loan repayments. It completely wrecked their economy. By the time the original reparations and interest were paid off, the place was basically destitute and trapped in a spiral of debt."[15] The legacy of debt combined with spates of corrupt leadership and natural disasters exacerbated by extreme resource exploitation have made Haiti the poorest country in the Western Hemisphere.

China also fell victim to debt as a technology of power more than once. By the turn of the twentieth century, Chinese social relations had been profoundly disturbed by the opium trade, recurrent war, and encroachments by commercial and Christian interests. Defeat in the first and second Opium Wars (1839–42 and 1856–60), the first Sino-Japanese War (1894–5), and the Boxer Rebellion (1900–1) not only brought national humiliation but increasing indemnities: "To pay the £30 million indemnity following the defeat by Japan, the Chinese were forced to make loans that cost them £100 million to repay. Likewise the $333 million Boxer indemnity required annual installment payments that absorbed almost all of the imperial government's income" (Stavrianos 1981: 325). To ensure repayment, colonial forces expropriated the post office and customs houses and essentially ran them as "debt collection agencies for foreign creditors" (King 2006: 665).[16] China continued to pay the indemnity to its colonial invaders until the chaos of the Second World War interrupted payments. Thus, before more sustained and organized forms of resistance to imperialism began after the Second World War, "national" debt was piled up by imperial administrators: (1) for investment projects typically related to the extraction of resources, (2) for colonial administration including pacification of the population through trained and armed professionals, and (3) by forcing weaker counterpart to accept punitive indemnities that they had little power to resist given alternative options.

Neocolonialism, the debt crisis, and neoliberalism

The social rights activist Desmond Tutu once intoned that "when the missionaries came to Africa they had the Bible and we had the land. They said 'Let us pray.' We closed our eyes. When we opened them we had the Bible and they had the land" (Gish 2004: 101). Tutu forgot to add that the Bible came with a "national" debt. As we will argue in this section, the "national" debt is a technology of power in permanent operation and just as effective as the Gatling gun in acting as a forcing house for the world market of differential accumulation and capitalist power.

Given the violence mobilized against anticolonial independence movements, there is considerable evidence to suggest that imperial powers were not rushing to relinquish their colonial possessions. However, the savagery of the Second World War left former colonial powers significantly weakened, only to find that the world they once ruled had shifted toward the United States and a weakened, but industrialized, Soviet Union. The moral or ethical landscape, albeit slowly and never entirely, was also transforming, making it more difficult to rule by brute force alone. Still, counter-revolutionary assassinations and violence of unimaginable proportions were inflicted upon independence leaders, social activists, and revolutionary movements in the hope of maintaining a world order for capitalist power that had been forged for centuries (Marcuse 1972; Blum 2004; Prashad 2007; Shaw 2011). According to Stavrianos, the shift toward decolonization after the Second World War "did not signify that independent status was granted gratuitously or indiscriminately" (1981: 665). He argues that three factors played a role in the timing of decolonization: (1) the economic and military power of the imperialist country—the stronger the country the more likely it could grant political independence while maintaining economic control; (2) the role of the United States and the Soviet Union and their level of involvement through war, technical advice, or the sale of arms; and (3) the political aims of the groups vying for independence—the more socially revolutionary, the more these forces were met with "extreme repressive measures" (Stavrianos 1981: 665–666). Since the creation of the United Nations, eighty former colonies have been granted formal political independence.[17] But for most countries, nothing profound had radically changed in their economic situations. If we are to believe Stavrianos, the wave of decolonization and political independence experienced after the Second World War was really played out on the international stage twice. The first time after Latin American nations gained their independence in the nineteenth century, and the second, when the peoples of Africa, Asia, and parts of the Asia-Pacific received theirs in the twentieth century (1981: 177ff and 623ff). But if the newly decolonized of both centuries were now politically independent, their national debt told an altogether different story: one of continued foreign domination by the owners of Anglo-American banks. In other words, the price tag for independence was the acceptance of a quantifiable national debt to be diligently serviced, largely by earning foreign exchange through international trade (Nyerere 1985).[18] For those not blinded by or serving imperial control, this new articulation of power was labeled neocolonialism by Kwame Nkrumah (1965). Stavrianos marked out the subtle difference between the two systems of rule: "if colonialism is a system of direct domination by the application of superior power, then neocolonialism is a system of indirect domination that cedes political independence in order to preserve economic dependence and exploitation" (Stavrianos 1981: 456). Economic dependence and exploitation is anchored, we argue, in the structural power of the national debt largely amassed and owed in foreign currency. One particularly revealing example arrived just before 1994 and the transformation to majority rule in apartheid South Africa. The elite white minority and transnational creditors feared that the African National Congress (ANC) was largely an unknown quantity with an overly progressive social agenda. The privileged whites dreaded the possibility of high taxes for reparations, rampant inflation due to social spending, and a redistribution of wealth from whites to blacks and the rich to the poor. To overcome these threats and to appease international and domestic creditors, the ANC agreed to tie its hands while in power. The chief way this was done was by agreeing to a loan from the International Monetary Fund that was, according to Bond, not needed. The real purpose of the loan was to ensure policy continuity:

> In December 1993, the first act of the Transitional Executive Committee (a government-in-waiting combining the ANC and the ruling National Party) was to borrow $850 million from the IMF, ostensibly for drought relief, although the drought had ended 18 months earlier. The loan's secret conditions were leaked to *Business Day* in March 1994, presumably to establish confidence in financial markets that the election in April 1994 and the subsequent transfer of power would be

characterized by a continuity in economic policy. These conditions included...lower import tariffs, cuts in state spending, large cuts in public-sector wages...[and]...intense pressure by IMF managing director Michel Camdessus to reappoint both finance minister Derek Keys and Reserve Bank governor Chris Stals, the two main stalwarts of National Party neo-liberalism. (Bond 2003: 68)

What this passage suggests is that debt was applied as a technology of power to ensure budgetary restraint and IMF supervision over the new government's fiscal policy. Not only did the ANC assume the national debt of the old apartheid regime—*debts that had been accumulated, in part, to repress and at times terrorize the African population*—but the ANC sacrificed its own program of reconstruction and development aimed at ameliorating the deplorable conditions experienced by the majority of its citizens disempowered by decades of racist rule (Cheru 2001). South Africa, however, is not alone in having its fiscal hands tied thanks to the national debt, the power of international capital markets, and IMF surveillance.

The use of debt as a technology of power was intensified in the post–Second World War era when, influenced by the world religion of "development," governments were encouraged to borrow to finance industrialization, infrastructure, and foreign-made arms (Rist 2008: 21). As George (1988: 21ff) notes, the military hardware imported by the Third World was typically used by privileged elites to repress their own populations. In other words, debt contributed to the militarization of the developing world. According to Stavrianos, the debt load of developing countries skyrocketed from "$19 billion in 1960, to $64 billion in 1970 and to $376 billion in 1979" (1981: 448). Today there are 129 developing countries accountable to the World Bank's Debt Reporting System. Using data from 2010, their total external stock of debt is now $4 trillion, up from $1.9 trillion in 1995 despite some cancellation of debt through the Heavily Indebted Poor Country initiative of the 2000s. Brazil, Russia, India, and China account for 40 percent of all external debt. Not surprisingly, the yearly interest charge has risen from $85 billion in 1995 to $155 billion in 2010 (World Bank 2012: 40). If we include principal repayments, the developing world collectively paid $582 billion to their creditors in 2010, up from $205 billion in 1995. Put simply, not only do the debts owed to foreign creditors continue to mount but so do the interest payments: they are perpetual and rising. In his revealing exposé on economic hit men, John Perkins suggests that this was exactly the point of clandestine US policy in the postwar world: entice foreign leaders into accepting debts so large that future governments would be *forever* unable to repay them (2004: xi). This debt not only enriched the owners of American firms in engineering, construction, oil and gas, and arms manufacturing but they also, insofar as the loans were made in US dollars, gave the US government and its corporations significant leverage over indebted countries across the world (Henry 2003). But this did not just happen by economic hit men and private bankers extending excessive loans to foreign governments. The mountain of debt that triggered the Third World Debt Crisis of the 1980s was intensified by massive inflation in oil prices and US interest rates (George 1988: 27ff). While the following discussion will be controversial for some, there is convincing evidence to suggest that this inflation was orchestrated and strategic rather than unforeseeable and accidental (Oppenheim 1976–7).

By the time the Second World War ended in 1945, the United States was the unquestionable global superpower. Not only did the United States come out of the war with its factories and businesses unharmed but warfare stimulated the domestic economy and attracted considerable foreign capital. By the end of the war, the United States was the largest creditor nation in the world. What also benefited the United States and the Allies were the massive onshore oil deposits found within the continental United States. Whereas Hitler effectively ran out of oil, the Allies swam to victory on a sea of American oil (Yergin 1992; Hayward 1995). As Yergin noted in his historical study of oil and international power, it was the First World War that focused strategic minds on the future of warfare and geopolitical power:

The Great War had made abundantly clear that petroleum had become
an essential element in the strategy of nations; and the politicians
and bureaucrats, though they had hardly been absent before, would
now rush headlong into the center of the struggle, drawn into the
competition by a common perception—that the postwar world would
require ever-greater quantities of oil for economic prosperity and
national power. (1992: 185)

The connection between oil, economic development, and international
power is well understood despite the resource curse literature and
mounting environmental contradictions. While fossil fuel energy is not
a sufficient cause for development, it is certainly necessary and vital
for economic growth (UNDP 2000; Wrigley 2010). Until the 1970s,
the United States had it in spades. How oil plays a special role in the
international monetary order is of crucial importance for our analysis
of debt as technology of power.

By at least 1944, the Allies were more or less assured of victory
against the Axis powers and started to prepare for international
commerce in the postwar order. At a conference in Bretton Woods
New Hampshire, plans were developed for an International Bank
for Reconstruction and Development (commonly referred to as the
World Bank). The bank was to help with the reconstruction of Western
Europe, but as time went on, its remit widened to include "developing"
countries with lower GDP. The International Monetary Fund was also
created at the conference and was tasked with facilitating global trade
by financing, what were thought to be at the time, temporary balance
of payment deficits. Because of the long history of Europeans coveting
gold as the only "real" money and the fact that most of the gold of the
world had amassed in the United States thanks to two world wars, a
new gold standard was proposed under IMF supervision. In this
scheme, the US dollar was pegged to gold at $35 dollars to one troy
ounce. In turn, member states of the IMF pegged their currencies to
the US dollar at a relatively fixed and stable rate. Many believed that
these fixed rates would help eliminate currency risk for international
business and therefore facilitate corporate planning and economic

growth. This system did not last long, however. The reason was that, in some senses, the United States never stopped fighting the Second World War. Primarily as a result of its prolonged war in Indochina, the country started to experience routine balance of payments deficits by the early 1970s. The United States was moving fast at becoming the world's largest debtor nation with twin deficits in its current and budget accounts. France was the first to realize that the United States had flooded the world with so many dollars that it did not have enough gold to back the currency in circulation. When Britain asked to cash in its reserves for gold, the Nixon administration unilaterally severed the link between the dollar and gold. The administration understood that the dollar had effectively become the world's reserve currency so that a "pure capitalist credit-money system" was virtually inevitable given the contradictions of the dollar (Ingham 2004: 77–78; see also Konings 2011: 89ff). How the Nixon administration managed this situation and the controversy surrounding it is of considerable interest from the perspective of debt as a technology of power.

US strategists not only knew that the dollar was the *de facto* world's reserve currency but also understood that demand for the currency would remain high given the size of the US securities market, financial innovation by Wall Street and in Eurodollar market, and the fact that a range of internationally traded commodities were denominated in US dollars (Konings 2011: 123). The most important commodity was, of course, oil—the essential ingredient needed by all nations to propel industrial development and a "modern" consumer economy (Clark 2005: 30). By 1971 or so, the production of conventional oil in the United States had peaked, so it was incredibly important for the United States, as a growing debtor nation, that oil remain denominated in dollars rather than a basket of currencies as some Middle Eastern bureaucrats thought to do (Spiro 1999: 110). Saudi Arabia agreed to keep the numeraire for crude petroleum in dollars and the Organization for Petroleum Exporting Countries (OPEC) followed suit. By 1973, the price of oil skyrocketed and by the end of 1974 was up by 400 percent. While orthodox history blames this increase in oil prices on the Arab oil embargo that followed the Yom Kippur War, there is substantial evidence to suggest that the price increase was desired by the Nixon administration and that Kissinger did his best to facilitate the war between Israelis, Syrians, and Egyptians by misrepresenting intentions to all parties (Oppenheim 1976–7; Kubursi and Mansur 1994: 313–327; Gowan 1999: 21–22; Engdahl 2004: 136; Clark 2005: 30).[19] Even if some scholars do not want to contemplate the notion that oil prices were strategically rigged, the effects of the 850 percent increase in the cost of oil from 1973 to 1980 are rather clear: (1) petrodollars flooded into major US banks and the City of London due to the weak financial system in the Middle East; (2) this had the effect of recapitalizing the major banks, allowing them to loan more funds abroad while at the same time financing the current account deficit of the United States; (3) a portion of these petrodollars were used to purchase US treasuries (thereby helping to drain reserves) and considerable amounts of military hardware, which further militarized the Middle East; (4) the price increase plunged the industrial economies into a period of stagflation—a condition of rising prices, slow growth, and high unemployment;[20] and finally (5) the price increase made oil much more expensive for countries with weaker currencies (Gowan 1999: 21–22; Clark 2005: 30ff).

Although economists have debated the source of the Great Inflation of the 1970s, it is pretty clear from the data that the massive inflation in the cost of oil was tightly correlated with the drastic increases in the consumer price index.[21] Seemingly to combat inflation, Paul Volcker, then chairman of the Federal Reserve, took a radical step and raised the federal funds rate to astonishing levels—as high as 21 percent.[22] The interest rate became a weapon. Unemployment climbed, but by 1983 inflation started to sink. We have little space for a full investigation here, but it is worth asking a question, keeping in mind that the price of oil was the main driver of inflation: how does increasing the cost of money do anything whatsoever to quell oil prices? If anything, high interest rates *would have made the cost of oil far more expensive* for those countries who had to borrow dollars to purchase oil. And this is precisely what happened to countries of the developing world dependent on oil imports: they had to borrow to meet their oil needs. In other words, these counties now had to pay not only the inflated cost of oil but the inflated cost plus interest on debts incurred from oil! The Volcker Shocks are all the more troubling when Nitzan's empirical research has convincingly demonstrated that economic growth and inflation are *inversely* correlated historically (Nitzan 2001: 253ff). In other words, in boosting interest rates to epic proportions, the Federal Reserve was helping to increase inflation rather than defeat it. This is a fact consistent with the basic math of interest tables for debt and in line with Rowbotham's (1998) claim that broad inflation is the result of a debt-based monetary system. The reason is simple: businesses ultimately push the cost of borrowing onto customers, increasing the price of goods and services. Lucky for Volcker, with unemployment skyrocketing, the beginning of a merger boom, and oil prices coming down in the early 1980s, inflation started to abate in the capitalist heartland and the financial press lionized him. But if things were returning to "normal" in the United States, the Volcker Shocks had served to inflate the debt of virtually every developing country—countries that often had to take new loans just to service mounting interest payments (George 1988; Hall 1988: 12). Usury used to be applied at the level of the individual, but it was now being applied at the level of entire populations as a permanent technology of imperial power. From the perspective of capital as power, interest is a weapon of redistribution, pure and simple, and the "debt crisis," exacerbated uncontrollably by heavy interest rates, was to serve as probably the greatest redistribution scheme in world history. The mirror image of it is found at the micropolitics of everyday debt in the credit card industry where banks prefer revolvers: customers who service their minimum monthly payments but never pay off their cards in full. Just like developing countries have to take out new loans to service old debts (therefore always increasing the total debt burden), so too do individuals take on new credit cards to service old ones. In this way, interest becomes perpetual, precisely the design of the first *permanent* "national" debt under the supervision of the Bank of England.[23] Whatever the exact design of the US Treasury and Federal Reserve during the Volcker Shocks, the idea that the persons running these institutions did not know that elevating interest rates to such proportions would exacerbate a debt crisis in the developing world is patently untenable. An important piece of evidence to this effect is the fact that in the debt crisis of the 1980s, the US administration "intervened heavily to prevent [debt restructuring or default] by offering financial assistance to bail out private investors and by tying this assistance to the adoption of tough IMF structural adjustment programmes in debtor countries" (Helleiner 2005: 952). And this brings us to what we call the debt–neoliberalism–restructuring nexus.

The literature on neoliberalism is vast and cuts across the social sciences. In such a short work like this, we cannot hope to fully engage the literature here. However, we share Cahill's analysis that the turn toward neoliberalism cannot be fully explained by policy makers grabbing on to a new set of ideas inspired by Hayek, Friedman, a legion of right-wing think tanks, and the Chicago School more generally (Cahill 2013; Cahill 2014). Our hypothesis is that insofar as neoliberalism can be conceived of as a set of policy prescriptions akin to the Washington Consensus, as coined and enumerated by Williamson (1990: 5–20), its origins are fundamentally rooted in the debt-based monetary system.[24] This is why—we suggest—*that despite the Keynesian interlude, there are so many points of contact between austerity, expropriation, dispossession, environmental exploitation, the oppression of workers and the obsession with economic growth in the capitalist past and present.* The differential accumulation of power in a debt-based money system constantly requires redistribution from debtors to creditors—be they individuals, nondominant corporations, or entire nation-states. The debt crisis that began in the 1980s and the debt crisis currently in the capitalist heartland are evidence of this fact insofar as entire political-economies have been and are daily being restructured as debt-repayment machines with: (1) drastic cuts in social spending and the sack of public workers; (2) newly minted and increasing "user fees" for public services; (3) the privatization of public assets; (4) increases in taxes for the majority (mostly indirect, so applied regressively); (5) the creation of special export zones to encourage foreign investment in cheap labor; and (6) the wholesale destructions of environments and ecosystems that take place when nature is commodified to pay back debt. The crucial thing to note is that, despite all these measures, more debt is forever piling on. In the next chapter we explore some of the most important consequences of debt as a technology of power in greater detail.

Consequences:
The Debt–Growth–Inequality Nexus

Nowadays, economic growth is heralded as the ultimate goal by so many governments. To an extent, this goal is forced upon society as it struggles to meet the interest charges on its debt. Whilst debt grows at compound interest towards infinity, in the physical world everything depreciates towards zero. I propose that the price we shall all pay for running this unwinnable race against compound interest is a polluted and depleted world. (Tarek El Diwany 1997: 189)

Over 300 years ago, as we've detailed, a country the size of the state of Minnesota or half the size of Papua New Guinea embarked on a financial experiment dictated largely by debts accrued in war that arguably succeeded in making it the richest and most powerful country in the world. Dozens of other countries tried to emulate its success with varying degrees of success and failure. But by granting the right to the Bank of England to print and issue money as debt, the Government of Britain delivered to them the equivalent of the philosopher's stone, enabling private citizens to create wealth with the stroke of a pen. Some 321 years later we are in a position to evaluate the consequences of that experiment. It is certainly true that the financial system that evolved out of that beginning has created, for some, great wealth and numerous technological marvels. The human life span has been extended and cures for disease and illness realized for considerable portions of the global population. We can only speculate how history would have changed if, for example, the Government of England had reserved the right to issue money to itself, and had other countries, such as the United States, later followed suit.

Regardless, issuing money as debt, as we have described above, not only creates hardships for individuals and countries unable to service or pay off their debts. We have tried to take that a little further and outline how debt is central to the global political economy as it has evolved since the fundamental institutional innovation of the Bank of England. As we have illustrated, it has been used as a means of expropriation of resources, a mode of discipline and market subjectification, and an instrument of control (Schild 2000).

Furthermore, for debt to be maintained and extended as a technology of power requires, as we noted earlier, perpetual and exponential economic growth. It is not incorrect to say that the requirement for growth arose simultaneously with the creation of a national debt, for without growth (or rapid inflation), the interest and/or dividend paid to debt holders could never be realized (Ferguson 2001: 140). Throughout history there have been periodic financial collapses when the necessary return to creditors was not forthcoming (Kindleberger and Aliber 2005; Reinhart and Rogoff 2009). Indeed, the current crisis in the Eurozone is attributable to fears of default related to the prospects for economic growth in some European countries.

Without perpetual and exponential growth, in other words, a debt-based monetary system cannot be sustained; furthermore, the rate of growth experienced over the past three centuries could not have been maintained without the fortuitous availability of affordable energy, first in the form of coal and then in the form of oil and gas.

In sum, we suggest that the ownership, production, and allocation of "capitalist credit money" creates a particular form of political economy that requires perpetual economic growth under the logic of differential accumulation, along with the availability of affordable fossil fuels to drive the necessary systems of production and consumption. We claim that this system is not natural and inevitable but a historical creation intertwined with the power of the 1%—of whom, owners and managers of financial institutions are the most important. We see the pursuit of this logic as leading toward what Polanyi called a "stark utopia"—a general situation of increasing austerity and hardship for ordinary families and ever-greater environmental despoliation. However, unlike Polanyi, we do not understand the emergence of this "stark utopia" as being generated by belief in "self-adjusting markets" but fundamentally rooted in our debt-based money system capitalized and owned by the few. Moreover, given the precarious state of existence for many, mounting and variegated expulsions from society, and despoiled or newly barren environments in many parts of the globe, we can already start to identify what might be called a geography of "stark utopias" (Bauman 2004; Davis 2007; Standing 2011; Sassen 2014). Being the children of the oil age, neoliberals claim that growth is the source of all well-being and assume the growth logic as self-evidently desirous. However, their general confusion over the monetary system, a child-like belief in "free markets," and their outlandish conviction in limitless growth lead them to ignore how debt serves as a technology of dispossession and private accumulation. This is an ongoing process that produces an ever-greater centralization of power as well as mounting environmental harm in spite of neoliberal incantations to the contrary that growth will promote individual freedoms and greater well-being.

In the remainder of this chapter, we will argue that we cannot fully evaluate the results of the debt-money experiment without considering our environmental decline, growing differential power and economic inequality, and a host of other social problems that stem from the debt-driven requirement for perpetual economic growth that is, in turn, made possible only by the availability of affordable energy. We will first examine briefly the history of the growth paradigm and the dilemmas that it poses. Then we will examine why maintaining the necessary rate of growth becomes more difficult, and why it necessitates yet more debt and the continuing acceleration of environmental degradation and differential power accumulation. Then, we will reconsider Thomas Piketty's (2014) work by examining the acceleration of differential power or inequality in light of our analysis of debt as a technology of power. More specifically, we will extend our analysis from the previous chapter on the role of debt in wealth transfer. Finally, we want to suggest the difficulties of changing our present environmental, political, and social trajectories within the existing political economy by briefly examining the question of who controls the future of food and energy.

A brief history of perpetual growth

As mentioned above, the prime assumption of neoliberal economists, policy makers, and politicians is that *perpetual economic growth, as measured by gross national product (GNP), is the source of all well-being and progress* (see Korten 1995: 70).[1] As Michel Foucault put it, for neoliberalism "there is only one true and fundamental social policy: economic growth" (Foucault 2004: 144; see also Gellner 1983; O'Connor 1998). Embedded in this logic is the assumption that we live in a world in which it is possible to expand our economies *ad infinitum*, and that, as Igoe and Brockington put it, "the world is a pie that can grow bigger and bigger until everyone can have a piece" (2007: 434; see also Arndt 1978: 143–144).

The computation of growth as "gross national product" was developed in the United States by Simon Kuznets and associates during the Great Depression (Fioramonti 2013: 23). With the memory of the 1930s depression fresh, leading economists such as John Maynard Keynes suggested that full employment was possible only in conditions of steady growth (Arndt 1978: 35). W. Arthur Lewis (1955: 420–421), in his classic work, *The Theory of Economic Growth*, suggested that growth would solve the problems of inflation and the balance of payments, promote greater economic equality, and provide greater control of the environment. Economic growth, some claimed, would even increase levels of happiness. As Paul Samuelson (1964: 778) suggested in the sixth edition of his famous text, *Economics*, while material goods are not themselves important, a society is happier when growing and not stagnating. Benjamin Friedman (2005) argues that economic growth fosters greater opportunity, tolerance of diversity, social mobility, commitment to fairness, and dedication to democracy; in other words, more money makes people more moral.[2]

Concerns about economic growth and its formal computation intensified after the Second World War and is perhaps now the world's largest religion (Hamilton 2004).[3] This religion is rationalized by the proposed benefits that include, among others things, increased national security, full employment, greater social and economic equality, increased social mobility, the economic development of the Third World, the growth of democracy, and greater happiness.[4] This is why during the Global Financial Crisis the solution was to chase more growth. As the editorial board of the *Financial Times* (2009) spelled out in its "survival plan for global capitalism,"

> There is one certainty. While recessions are inevitable, deep depressions or slumps—or whatever you call them—are neither necessary nor welcome. They destroy wealth, sap happiness and crush old certainties. What is more, increasing poverty is a grave threat to world stability and democracy. Revolutions often start as bread riots, and economically-stagnant countries make belligerent neighbours. Growth must be restarted.

Regardless of the origins of the need for perpetual growth and the ideology required to sustain it, one cannot argue that historically the goal has not met with remarkable success. As Angus Maddison (2001) documents in his monumental work, *The World Economy: A Millennial Perspective*, economic growth was virtually absent until the nineteenth century, when it surged in the era of abundant, affordable, and relatively accessible fossil fuels (Smil 1994; Goldstone 2002; Wrigley 2010) (see Figure 4.1).

Currently global GDP is over $70 trillion and has grown at an annual rate of about 2.5 percent since 1750. Since 2000, the rate of growth has been about 3 percent, which is the minimum that economists consider necessary for a "healthy" economy.

Of course, the drive to growth also led to unprecedented global competition for resources, two world wars, hundreds of smaller-scale conflicts, and the expenditure of untold lives and wealth, not to mention mountains of debt at different scales of global society. Yet

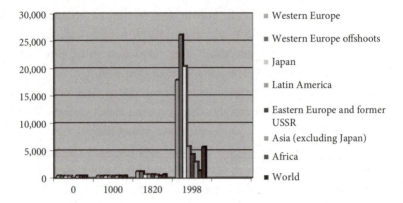

Figure 4.1 Rate of per capita GDP growth from 0 to 1998 AD by regions

Source: Adapted from Maddison, Angus (2001) *The World Economy: A Millennial Perspective* (Paris: Development Centre of the Organization for Economic Co-operation and Development).

the assumption that growth could solve socioeconomic and political problems persisted and ultimately became the main policy objective of virtually every country in the world as the system of national accounts and the discourse of "development" was institutionalized in the United Nations at the end of the Second World War (Rist 2008; Fioramonti 2013: 32).[5]

Other than the separation of economics from politics and the mathematization of the economy as a distinct sphere of "formal" study, the insistence on perpetual growth is the key belief that distinguishes classical economic theory from its neoliberal variant. Classic economists such as Adam Smith, John Stuart Mill, John Maynard Keynes, and, more recently, Amartya Sen did not envision perpetual economic growth as a specific policy goal. They saw political economy and later economics providing the tools for economies to grow to a certain point as organisms do in nature, and then, when people could, in Keynes words, live "wisely, agreeably and well," growth would level off (see Jackson 2009: 41–42; Skidelsky 2009: xvii).

There is of course little doubt that some degree of economic growth for a given time period may have positive social benefits. However, there are major problems with pursuing economic growth for its own sake in perpetuity.[6] First, the computation is merely an adding up of economic transactions in the economy. What this means is that things that actually harm society—like car accidents, more disease, oil spills, and so on—are actually added to GDP. Second, economic growth tells us very little about how the potential benefits and harms of our transactions are distributed across and between societies. Moreover, it is difficult to justify empirically whether perpetual growth, the keystone of neoliberal logic, has delivered on its claims. If we go back only to 1950, the global economy has expanded more than six-fold (see Maddison 2001: 125). Surely with that much growth, we should have seen considerable improvement in the promised social, economic, environmental, and political gains. Yet nationally and internationally we are more unequal than ever (see, e.g., Noah 2012; Stiglitz 2012; Dorling 2014; Johnston 2014; Di Muzio 2015); in the United States alone, one in five children still lives in poverty; instead of increasing, social mobility is decreasing (Bradbury 2011); most developing countries are so heavily in debt that funds that should go to build roads, hospitals, schools, and public health facilities and to reduce poverty are flowing into Western banks and financial institutions just to service the interest on the debts. World expenditure on armaments has increased by 50 percent since 2001 alone (Shah 2012), so it is difficult to make the case that growth has led to greater national security. Politically our institutions are increasingly dominated by large corporations and financial institutions. Moreover, as Bill McKibben (2007) points out, while in 1946, the United States was the happiest country among four advanced economies, thirty years later it declined to being ranked eighth among eleven advanced countries, and a decade later it ranked tenth among twenty-three countries, which include countries from the developing world. Furthermore, there is a steady decline in the percentage of Americans who claim their marriages are happy, are satisfied with their jobs, or find pleasure in the place they live. In fact, overall in the United States, there has been a dramatic drop in social capital, that is, relations of cooperation, reciprocity, and trust (Putnam 2000).

While neoliberal economists generally accept a view of the world whereby problems can be solved through the perpetual growth of the economy, there have been periodic dissenters within the field of economics, skeptical of the benefits of rampant economic growth (Mishan 1967; Scitovsky 1976). The most renown is perhaps Herman Daly.

In 1996, Daly, a former economist with the World Bank, published his seminal work, *Beyond Growth: The Economics of Sustainable Development*. He not only argued that growth was unsustainable, but that it was doing irreparable harm to our societies, as well as our environments, and that GDP, then at just over $9 trillion in the United States, was an irresponsible way to measure the progress of a society.

Yet by 2014 US GDP was almost $17 trillion, or seventeen times greater than it was in 1967 and eight times greater than it was in 1976. Global GDP stood at about $70 trillion, over twenty times what it was in 1967, and almost twice the size it was when Daly issued his warning. In fact, if the US economy grew at the minimum desired rate of 3 percent real GDP growth a year[7] (close to the growth rate of Japan from 1900 to 2000), in 2100 the GDP, that is what US citizens are consuming and producing, would be over $200 trillion, or 600 times what they spent and produced in 1950! And since some emerging nations tend to grow at higher rates than wealthy nations, global GDP could *theoretically* approach or exceed a quadrillion dollars.[8]

While neoliberal economists assume that more growth is better, it is impossible to conceive of the effects of a quadrillion dollar global economy on the world's ecosystems, even if it was possible, let alone their societies. As John Magnus Speth (2008: x) argues, even if our economic output remained at its *present* level, the world would be virtually uninhabitable by the end of this century. The damage that has been and is being done is well documented by J. R. McNeill (2000), among many others, and illustrated pictorially by Will Steffen et al. (2004: 132–134) and his associates in the series of charts detailing the exponential environmental effects of economic growth (see Figure 4.2).[9]

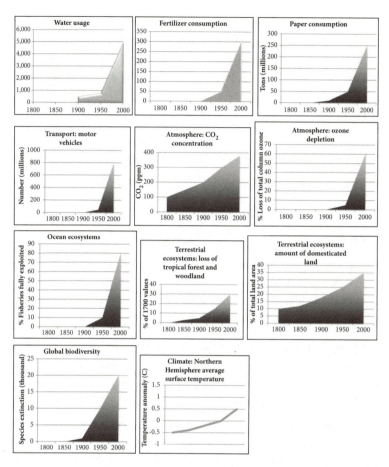

Figure 4.2 Rates of resource extraction and environmental change

Source: Adapted from Steffen, W., et al. (2004) *Global Change and the Earth System: A Planet under Pressure* (New York: Springer): 132–133.

Even environmental economists are hard-pressed to come up with a scenario in which it would be possible to maintain growth and yet limit environmental destruction. Tim Jackson, economics commissioner on the UK Sustainable Development Commission, notes that "…there is as yet no credible, socially just, ecologically sustainable scenario of continually growing income for a world of 9 billion people." Furthermore,

Resource efficiency, renewable energy and reductions in material throughput all have a vital role to play in ensuring the sustainability of economic activity. But the analysis…suggests that it is entirely fanciful to suppose that deep emission and resource cuts can be achieved without confronting the structure of market economies. (Jackson 2009: 86)

Jackson is one of the few environmental economists examining the impact of economic growth on the environment, who recognizes that slowing or stopping growth will itself lead to economic disaster; that is, while continued growth will destroy the environment, stopping or slowing it will destroy the economic foundations of our societies. He concludes,

Taking a step back for a moment, there are only two ways out of [the dilemma of growth]. One is to make growth sustainable, the other is to make de-growth stable. Anything else invites either economic or ecological collapse. (Jackson 2009: 128)

But there is another problem that is equally, if not more, sobering: *as economies generate more debt and material goods, as they grow wealthier, it becomes more and more difficult for them to sustain growth.* Economists inexplicably call this the "convergence factor," noting that developing countries, which are able to maintain higher growth rates, will "converge" to the growth rate of advanced economies (Jones 2002: 63ff; Barro and Xavier Sala-i-Martin 2004: 462–463). But this makes little sense as an explanation for differential growth rates; more accurately, the reason has to do with the nature of exponential growth.

From the investment side, maintaining a compound rate of growth, as David Harvey (2010: 216) notes, requires money managers to find more and more profitable investment opportunities. Currently there is almost $100 trillion controlled by institutional investors in pensions and insurance alone, an amount that has more than doubled since 2000 (OECD 2014: 7, 9). In physical terms, as Harvey puts it,

When capitalism was made up of activity within a fifty-mile radius around Manchester and Birmingham in England and a few other hotspots in 1750, then seemingly endless capital accumulation at a compound rate of 3 percent posed no big problem. But right now think of endless compound growth in relation not only to everything that is going on in North America, Oceania and Europe, but also east and south-east Asia as well as much of India and the Middle East, Latin America and significant areas of Africa. The task of keeping capitalism going at this compound rate is nothing if not daunting. (Harvey 2010: 27–28)

Harvey (2010: 28) notes that the wave of privatizations that is so central to neoliberal policy prescriptions is less about the unproven increases in efficiency and more about finding places to invest money and keep it working and growing. Furthermore, finding an exponential increase in places to grow money requires greater and greater risk, as the subprime mortgage fiasco proved.

To illustrate further the difficulty of maintaining growth, from the resource extraction side, from 1990 to 1995 the lumber industry in the United States maintained a growth rate over that period of about 3.5 percent by cutting down the equivalent of one and a half million more trees than they had in the previous five-year period. However, in order to maintain the same 3.5 percent growth rate from 2005 to 2010, they would have had to cut down the equivalent of two and a half million more trees (Howard 2007). Extrapolate those growth figures to automobiles, fish stocks, water usage, and so on, and the near impossibility of sustaining exponential growth becomes more easily apparent.

While we cannot elaborate further here, another significant consequence of the difficulty of growth maintenance is that the time spent and the processes used to maintain growth must accelerate; everything has to move faster.[10] Money has to flow faster, people have to work faster, and even our food crops and animals have to grow faster; by using growth hormones, antibiotics, and feed lots, for example, beef cattle now reach slaughter weight in fourteen months, instead of a natural three to four years (see Robbins 2005; Pollan 2007). Time becomes an enemy to be overcome (Gleick 2000).

We can conceptualize the difficulty of maintaining exponential growth, also, by remembering that capitalization is a claim on expected future earnings and that these earnings are contingent not only on the power of firms and certain government organs but also on the ability to commodify various aspects of the natural and social world. Furthermore, the transformation of the natural world into money and earnings requires energy, which is also beginning to approach limits and has severe consequences for the biosphere and human and natural life (Heinberg 2003; Rockström 2009; IPCC 2014). Chris Martenson (2011: 150) estimates that each 1 percent of economic growth requires a 0.27 percent increase in petroleum production; at a 4 percent growth rate, the world would need to increase the present 90 millions of barrels of oil a day to some 114 mbd by 2020. The problem is not necessarily with supply (although some estimates are that conventional oil is in decline), but with the environmental and monetary cost of retrieving what remains, including "unconventional" fossil fuels. In 1930 it took one barrel of oil to extract 100. By 1970, with oil more difficult to extract in certain regions, the ratio fell to 25:1; by the 1990s it was between 18:1 and 10:1. There may be lots of oil in tar sands or shale, but the ratio between usable energy and energy needed to extract it is about 3:1, 2:1, and, some argue, even less (Martenson 2011: 133ff).

Debt, growth, and austerity

When we consider statistics on debt, we have to remember that one person, corporation, or government's debt is another entity's asset. The financial sector runs on debt. That is their main product; and they market that product as aggressively as any other producer of goods and services. But unlike other products, which require labor and resources to create, financial assets are largely created by computer entries. And while we may marvel at the fact that a car can be built in eighteen hours, billions of dollars in financial assets can be created (or destroyed) in milliseconds.

This has one very significant implication: an economy operating with debt-money, and, therefore, one that requires perpetual and exponential growth, requires also the creation of evermore debt. But more debt, in turn, requires more growth to produce the required interest or dividend, and so the cycle continues. If at any point, the rate of growth is insufficient to produce the money required to pay debts, financial crisis inevitably ensues as credit collapses.

So while maintaining economic growth is not intrinsically good, particularly when weighed against the negative externalities it produces that include environmental devastation, the centralization of power, and dysfunctional social relations, growth (or, more accurately, capital accumulation) is necessary to ensure that the financial system does not freeze up or collapse and take the rest of the society with it. That is the price we pay and the dilemma we face for granting to private interests the right to issue money as interest-bearing debt.

Currently total global debt exceeds $199 trillion or almost 300 percent of global GDP (Reddy 2013; Dobbs et al. 2015).[11] If we assumed that the average interest on the debt was 5 percent with a term of ten years, the global economy would have to produce over that period over $50 trillion of new money in order to service all the interest. And that assumes that no new debt is issued, which is impossible in a debt-based monetary system. While we can only examine a few of the consequences of this process, we will focus, first, on how this plays out in loans to developing countries and, second, compare the process to some effects on domestic borrowers. Our major point here is that in a debt-based economy there can never be sufficient growth to honor all debt payments, and, furthermore, if growth accelerates, central banks will raise interest rates, not only increasing the need for growth to pay the additional interest, but paradoxically, making growth more difficult by reducing economic activity and job creation. Consequently, the money required for financial institutions to receive their needed return on capital must be realized elsewhere. In brief, what leading economists and banks call "austerity" is, in reality, a "taking" from others.

Odious debt

We noted earlier how, after the withdrawal of colonial powers, loans were extended to now nominally independent colonies as a means of discipline, market subjectification, and control. It is difficult to imagine how lending institutions, including the World Bank, could have assumed that there could ever be sufficient growth in those countries to produce the revenue to pay off the debts. Consider, only, that it required the control of the resources of over half the world, along with the control of a source of cheap energy for the wealthy countries of the world to maintain their necessary growth rate in the nineteenth and twentieth centuries, and it is easily apparent how absurd it was to expect colonial and ex-colonial countries to collectively grow sufficiently to pay off their debts. This is one among other reasons we can call it *odious debt*.

The term "odious debt" originates with the Russian jurist Alexander Sack and refers to a type of sovereign debt generally assumed by dictatorial regimes where the borrowed money did not benefit the citizenry (and is often used to repress them), where the citizenry did not consent to the debt, and where creditors had full knowledge of the situation (UNCTAD 2007; Bonilla 2011). In 1997, when Franjo Tudjman of Croatia eliminated political opponents and looted public funds, the IMF cut off lending to Croatia. But commercial banks, nevertheless, lent an additional $2 billion to the Tudjman government until his death in 1999. While these loans benefited virtually no one but corrupt government officials and the banks that extended the loans, they, nevertheless, had to be repaid, usually by cutting funds for education, sanitation, health, and poverty reduction. Similar loans were made to the Apartheid government of South Africa, to dictators in Nigeria, Philippines, Nicaragua, Haiti, and much of Latin America, the financial burden of which is borne by the citizens of those countries, for which they not only received little if any benefit but with which many were imprisoned, tortured, and killed (Kremer and Jayachandran 2002; Ndikumana and Boyce 2011).

This pattern of too much money being invested in countries that could not possibly produce the revenue to honor the loans has been repeated all over the world over the past forty years, with everyone pointing the blame for the debt crisis at everyone else.

However, these sovereign debts represent a colossal failure of banking judgment, ignorance of economic theory, or more than likely, as we mentioned earlier, a cynical strategy for economic and political control. To put these loans and the conditionalities that have been imposed on most countries by the IMF in perspective, imagine yourself going to the bank for a loan to open a hardware store on Main Street. The bank, your only source of capital, extends the loan but sets these conditions: you must pay back the loan with currency having half the value of the amount you received, essentially doubling your debt burden, and, if you borrow any additional money, you must pay twice the interest rates of competitors. In addition, the bank supports a big box store down the road from you and extends loans to a dozen other people to open hardware stores on your block, with whom you must compete. That essentially is what happens to emerging economies as conditions of the loans they have received. Unable to attain growth rates necessary to repay the loans, they have been forced, first, to restructure by devaluing their currency, ostensibly to encourage exports and discourage imports. Then, to counter inflation, they must pay higher interest rates on loans, and they must compete with economic sectors of developed economies that possess far superior technologies and whose businesses have lower energy costs. If you have a cup of morning coffee, remember that there are over fifty coffee-exporting countries in the world, most trying to produce and sell as much coffee as possible to pay their external debts. But the glut of coffee on the market drives down prices, making it more difficult to attain the economic growth necessary to pay even the interest on the debt (Pendergrast 1999: 277ff; Tucker 2011; Robbins 2013).[12] What is true of coffee is true also of most commodities (e.g., lumber, beef, tea, etc.), driving up the profits of importers, but leaving exporting countries even further in debt.

To make matters worse, not only is there no provision, beyond default, for countries to declare bankruptcy but also unpayable sovereign debts are being purchased by hedge fund traders at a fraction of their face value from banks that have given up on collecting. These traders—dubbed "vulture capitalists" by Wall Street traders themselves— generally seek payment for the full face value of the debt by taking countries to court.

The default by Argentina in 2014, its second in thirty years, is instructive (Sassen 2014). First, it should be noted that Argentina's external debt was accumulated by the military junta (1976–83) and, through the painstaking investigative work by Alejandro Olmos Gaona, was declared odious in Argentine court in 2000 (George 1988: 129–130; Naylor 1994: 142–149; Olmos Gaona 2001). When Argentina defaulted on its sovereign debt in 2001, Elliott Associates L.P., an investment firm headed by Paul Singer, purchased at a large discount, some $48 million of unpaid debts. Singer demanded from Argentina the full value of the debt, which, when interest and fees were added, was valued at anywhere from $1.5 billion to $3 billion. Singer took Argentina to court to collect, and a US federal judge ruled in Singer's favor, forcing Argentina to again default to avoid payment and throwing their economy into turmoil.[13] Singer had pioneered these funds, when, in October 1995, Elliott Associates purchased some $28.7 million of Panamanian sovereign debt for $17.5 million from large banks such as Citi and Credit Suisse, which had given up on ever collecting. As was normal in situations where countries did not have enough to service their debt, the government of Panama asked bondholders to restructure the debt, by extending the time period or taking a lower payment. Most agreed, but not Elliott Associates; they demanded full repayment of the $28.7 million plus interest and fees. Elliott filed a lawsuit against Panama in New York district court, and the case went all the way to the New York Supreme Court, which sided with Elliott. Panama had to pay the firm $57 million, with an additional $14 million going to other creditors.

Following Singer's innovation, other funds were formed, such as Dart Container Corp and EM Ltd., both linked to Kenneth Dart, one of the most famous names in the world of vulture funds, to purchase sovereign debt of other indebted countries and demand full payment of the debts.

The problem that has been raised has to do with the morality of these transactions. The money that is flowing to investors in these funds is money that is often being taken away from investments in education, health, and poverty alleviation in these countries (Palast 2014). Take the region of sub-Saharan Africa, for example. This region pays $10 billion every year in debt service. That is about four times as much money as the countries in the region spend on health care and education.

However, lest we place too much blame on the likes of Paul Singer and Kenneth Dart, we must remember that most of these loans were issued by major banks, often with formal or informal assurances by the International Monetary Fund or World Bank that the loans could be repaid.

Domestic (odious?) debt

However, debt as a technology of power has not only been used in developing countries; it is a technique and pattern that is being applied in developed countries as well, and may be as odious as the debt foisted upon the developing world. The parallels between the use of debt to discipline, subjugate, and control other countries and the use of debt to control the citizens of so-called developed countries are striking.

As with global debt, debts of all kinds have been increasing dramatically in the United States, as well as in other countries of the world (see Figures 4.3 and 4.4).

Since the vast majority of money is released into the economy as capitalized money bearing interest to the owners and managers of banks, this means that one way to expand earnings is by expanding the pool of debtors. One of the major inventions here was the creation and development of the consumer and various types of consumer credit "products"—from credit cards and lines of credit to car and home-equity loans. The result has been a dramatic increase in consumer debt (see Figure 4.5).

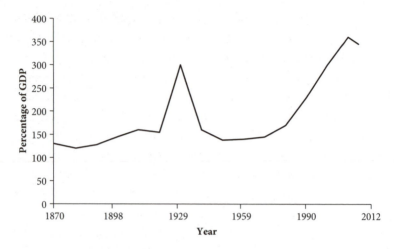

Figure 4.3 US private and public debt as a percent of GDP, 1870–2012

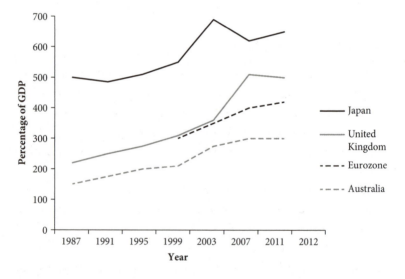

Figure 4.4 Total private and public debt as a percent of GDP: major countries

The literature on this topic is too vast to cover in any depth here, but at least three broad trends can be identified (Gelpi and Julien-Labruyère 2000; Manning 2001; Montgomerie 2006; 2009; 2013; Sassatelli 2007; Burton 2008; Leonard 2011; Robbins 2014: Chapter 1; Soederberg 2014).

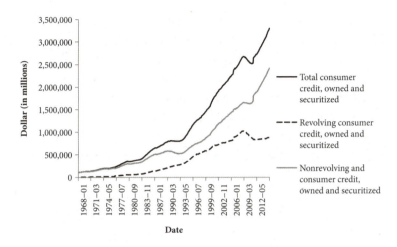

Figure 4.5 US consumer credit, 1968–2012 in $millions

Source: see http://www.federalreserve.gov/releases/g19/hist/cc_hist_mt_flows.html

First, creating the consumer through advertising has not only increased in geographical scope since the organized capitalization of advertising firms but also deepened across a range of new and traditional media. One indication has been the yearly growth in advertising spending, now surpassing a half trillion dollars—higher than the GDP of 163 countries listed by the World Bank.[14] This spending facilitates debt as a technology of power insofar as it is designed to produce forms of identity and subjectivity that often require access to consumer credit to achieve (Gill 1995). In a sense, advertisers have sold to consumers the same image of the good life that economic development advocates and lending agencies sold to citizens and politicians of the Third World.

Second, consumer credit instruments have globalized—albeit, extremely unevenly. One key example is the credit card industry, which views emerging economies as a key source of growth so long as consumer behavior can continue to be modified (Research and Markets; Global Credit Card Industry—Emerging Markets 2010). In China alone the market for credit cards grew by 13 percent in 2013 to 391 million cards, with Euromonitor predicting strong growth for plastic credit going forward (Waldmeir and Rabinovitch 2014).

Moreover, as wages have stagnated or fallen for the majority in mature economies, there has been an increasing reliance on consumer credit to finance necessities like food, medicine, and electricity—in part, what Soederberg calls "debtfarism" (2014). To be sure, some of this spending is on conspicuous consumption, but we must also recall that borrowers are not borrowing money that exists when they use bank products, but money created on computer screens. Furthermore, nonsecuritized loans account for $62 trillion dollars (McKinsey Global Institute 2013)—the largest category of debt in the world—while the World Bank notes that household consumption represents about 60 percent of global GDP. Without debt-financed spending, then, there is little doubt that crises would ensue.

Third, there is a burgeoning industry growing up around the consumer debt revolution that includes debt-collecting agencies, debt counselors, credit-rating agencies, subprime debt traders, pawn shops, new technologies to monitor debtor whereabouts, and new punitive legal frameworks including the return of incarceration for unpaid debts (Gill and Roberts in Young et al. 2011; LeBaron and Roberts 2012; Corkery and Silver-Greenberg 2014).

The number of people whose debts have been referred to collection agencies is huge: some 35 percent of all people in the United States with credit records have, at one time or another, been reported to collection agencies with unpaid debts averaging $5,178 (Boak 2014; Ratcliffe et al. 2014).

Whereas creditors in developed countries can launch into indebted countries their legal teams and, if necessary, their country's military to enforce debt payments, domestic banks and other lending institutions can send in lawyers, judges, and police.

For example, in the United States there is a growing market for bad debt, that is, debt that is more than a few months in arrears. Investors buy "bad paper," as it is called, at pennies on the dollar and then use every means, both legal and illegal, to collect.[15] Jake Halpern (2014) describes the world of the debt collector, individuals and firms who buy debts from banks that the banks have not been able to collect.

Often they buy these debts for as low as 0.04 on the dollar, reaping huge profits in the process. By law, banks are not able to count as assets debts that are 180 days or more in arrears. Banks then "charge off" these debts and then "sell" them in bulk to collectors who then attempt to collect from the debtors. These buyers are the domestic equivalents of "vulture capitalists."

The bad debt business really took off in the United States after the savings and loan crisis of the early 1990s, when the US government seized the assets of failed savings and loan institutions and auctioned off their unpaid loans. Debt buyers then call, threaten, and sue debtors to collect as much as they can. Halpern describes one portfolio of debt purchased by one bad paper collector for $28,000, that brought in more than $90,000 in six weeks, with the remaining unpaid loans then resold for $31,000, and resulting in an almost 200 percent return on the initial investment (2014: 15). The bad paper market grew from $582 million in 2009 to over one billion in 2012 (Hunter 2014). As a consequence, the number of lawsuits against consumers has skyrocketed, reaching 200,000 in New York State alone in 2011. Other problems include collectors buying portfolios that have been stolen or have already been sold to someone else, threats of violence, and so on. As Halpern documents, the bad paper collection industry often attracts the more unsavory elements of society. As one debt buyer who hired people to collect debts he had purchased described them to Halpern, "Oh my God, they were like thugs," but, he said, the more clean-cut types couldn't do the job (2014: 13).

Often the methods used to collect these debts are illegal. In 2015, New York State reached a settlement of $675,000 with one of the biggest debt buyers, the Encore Capital group, over the filing of thousands of flawed debt collection lawsuits against state residents (Silver-Greenberg 2015). And, as with indebted countries, to repay creditors domestic debtors must reduce spending on such family necessities as food, shelter, and health care.

While there are many other consequences of debt-based money, we will mention only two here. First, while it seems natural to say that we need to reduce our debt, we must recognize that reducing debt reduces the money supply. There are many who claim that global and domestic sovereign debt is too high and must be paid down. But doing so makes it harder for everyone else to repay his or her debts and could itself produce a financial crisis. That is, for every government debt there is a corresponding private asset, and if the debt is paid off, the asset in the form of interest-bearing securities is destroyed.

To a great extent, the argument over whether to decrease or increase government spending is rooted in the contradictory functions of debt-money. On the one hand, it serves as a *store of value*; consequently, holders of money deplore inflation because it reduces the value (or purchasing power) of the money held. On the other hand, money also serves as a *means of exchange*; consequently the more money (or debt) issued, the greater the amount of economic activity, and the more goods and services produced and jobs created. The fact that central banks have as their prime goal the control of inflation is indicative of who controls central banks—the holders of interest-bearing wealth.[16]

Second, there is a hierarchy of debt-owners, such that some receive their return on capital before others; that is, some creditors have priority over others. This is clearest in the case of sovereign debt. Greece, for example, unable to service its sovereign debt, carried out the biggest debt restructuring in history in 2012. Thanks to some €174.5 billion bailout money from other Eurozone governments, Greece was able to pay some of its creditors. But the Eurozone and the IMF required first paying Greek bondholders, and only using what was left for public needs, such as paying pensioners or teachers (Stevis 2013). The logic of this priority is that government bonds are generally considered the safest investment, and if bondholders faced the prospect of greater risk, bonds would cease to be as attractive an investment and more interest would be charged. But if growth is not maintained, debt is more difficult to repay, and more must be confiscated from other sources in order for the interest on the debt to be repaid to priority creditors. Various ways to do this include eliminating money for such things as education, welfare, and health services, as has been the case in developing countries. Generally such measures go under the term "austerity," and using a household metaphor, financiers, bankers, and co-opted politicians justify austerity by claiming that the indebted government or country is "living beyond its means," as if they were all members of one big household irresponsibly spending more than it earned. A more apt household metaphor, however, would be one in which one sibling among ten expropriated 50 percent of the family income, leaving the rest for his nine brothers and sisters. Furthermore, if the family income ever declined, he demanded to be reimbursed first when it increased again, insisting that his brothers and sisters give him a portion of their income if he suffered any loss.

Thus, as Pavlina R Tcherneva (2014) documents, over the past thirty years, in any economic downturn, as soon as growth returns, the wealthiest 10 percent receive their money first, and, more recently, even confiscated some of the income of the other 90 percent (see Figure 4.6).

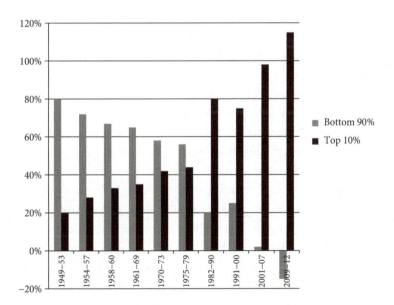

Figure 4.6 Distribution of average income during expansions

Source: Tcherneva, P.R. (2014) "Reorienting Fiscal Policy: A Bottom-up Approach," *Journal of Post-Keynesian Economics*, Vol. 37.

As Tcherneva puts it,

> An examination of average income growth during every postwar
> expansion (from trough to peak) and its distribution between the
> wealthiest 10 percent and bottom 90 percent of households reveals
> that income growth becomes more inequitably distributed with every
> subsequent expansion during the entire postwar period. *Only during
> the 1950–53 expansion did the bottom 90 percent capture all of the
> average income growth in the economy. Since then, the top 10 percent
> of households have been capturing a greater and greater share of the
> income growth and, in the latest expansion, they have captured over 115
> percent of the income growth, while incomes of the bottom 90 percent of
> households declined.* (2014: 54–55, our emphasis)

Inequality and the privileged decile

There is no question that inequality in the United States and elsewhere
has risen dramatically over the past forty years, as evidenced by the
number of recent works on the subject (see, e.g., Freeland 2012; Noah
2012; Stiglitz 2012; Dorling 2014; Johnston 2014; Di Muzio 2015).
Globally inequality has reached the level whereby the global 1% own
just under 50 percent of global wealth (Oxfam 2015).

Factors identified as responsible for this trend include rapid
technological change, the rapid globalization of the economy, stagnant
or declining wages, the growth of finance, and the weakening or outright
destruction of labor unions, particularly in the United States. The work
on differential capital accumulation that has received the most attention
is that of Thomas Piketty and Emmanuel Saez, particularly Piketty's
(2014) best-selling *Capital in the Twenty-First Century*, which purports
to show that growing inequality is endemic to a capitalist economy.

The idea that inequality is an intrinsic feature of our economic system
runs counter to the claim of neoliberal economists who, historically,
have maintained that growth will reduce inequality and the need for
wealth redistribution. In their view, increased wealth will "trickle down"
the economic ladder (Arndt 1978: 46–47; Kempf 2008). The key research
on which this claim was based was Simon Kuznets and Elizabeth Jenks

(1953) work, *Shares of Upper Income Groups in Income and Savings*. It was the first work to rely on income distribution statistics and the first to measure social inequality on such a large scale. Based on tax records between 1913 and 1948, the authors demonstrated that economic inequality dramatically decreased during that time, that the income of the top 10 percent went from 45–50 percent of national income to 30–35 percent. Kuznets and Jenks ostensibly had statistical proof that income inequality had dropped dramatically and that capitalism had widespread income benefits in the United States (Piketty 2014: 12–13).

Kuznets and Jenks recognized that the intervening World Wars and the Depression played a role in the lessening of income extremes; nevertheless, the study served as the foundation for economic policy over the next fifty years and the key justification for neoliberal austerity policies.

Piketty essentially replicated Kuznet and Jenk's study by extending the data back to the eighteenth century and forward to the present and into the future. His conclusion was that the normal process in a capitalist economy is for wealth and income divergence, that when, as he put it, the return on capital exceeds the rate of economic growth, as it has done for most of the past two centuries, wealth diverges and inequality increases. Figure 4.7 represents the historical trajectory of

The top decile share in US national income dropped from 45 to 50 percent in the 1910s–1920s to less than 35 percent in the 1950s (this is the fall documented by Kuznets); it then rose from less than 35 percent in the 1970s to 45–50 percent in the 2000s–2010s.

Figure 4.7 Income inequality in the United States, 1910–2010: percent of income earned by the top decile

Sources and series: see piketty.pse.fr/capital21c.

the income in the United States of the top 10 percent, while Figure 4.8 represents the share of income and wealth of the top 1 percent.

We briefly discussed Piketty's contributions in Chapter 1, and this is not a place for an extensive review of his monumental work. But his basic point is that when the rate of return on capital exceeds the rate of economic growth, capital will continue to amass a greater amount of the national income than labor. In essence, going back to our household metaphor, one sibling will continue to expropriate a far larger share of household income than his sisters and brothers. The question of whether or not the privileged child deserves that share is, of course, the stuff of monumental debate.[17] Our question is, how does he do it? For Piketty (2014: 26–27) the key is the role of inherited wealth. He argues,

> When the rate of return on capital significantly exceeds the growth rate of the economy (as it did through much of history until the nineteenth century and as is likely to be the case again in the twenty-first century), then it logically follows that inherited wealth grows faster than output and income. People with inherited wealth need only save a portion

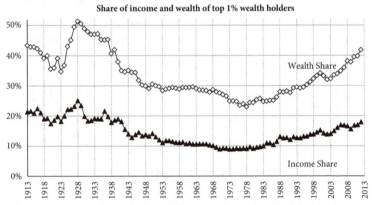

Since the 1980s the share of total household wealth owned by families in the top 1% of the wealth distribution has grown proportionally less than the share of total pre-tax national income earned by these families. Source: Appendix Tables B1 and B25. (Piketty 2014).

Figure 4.8 Income and wealth inequality in the United States, 1913–2012: percent of income earned and wealth held by the top 1 percent

Source: Thomas Piketty and Emmanuel Saez (2003) "Income Inequality in the United States, 1913–1998," Quarterly Journal of Economics, Vol. 118, No. 1. Updated to 2008 at http://emlab.berkeley .edu/users/saez. See more at: http://inequality.org/income-inequality/#sthash.XAUIRSwA.dpuf.

of their income from capital to see that capital grow more quickly than the economy as a whole. Under such conditions, it is almost inevitable that inherited wealth will dominate wealth amassed from a lifetime's labor by a wide margin, and the concentration of capital will attain extremely high levels—levels potentially incompatible with the meritocratic values and principles of social justice fundamental to modern democratic societies.

There is no question that inheritance, as Piketty suggests, plays a key role in inequality. But he neglects to discuss the role of debt-based money and the role of interest on debt in the global economy, and debt's role as a regressive tax. Where is this inherited wealth coming from? Debt, itself, as we've mentioned, is a technology of wealth transfer that essentially divides the population into those who are net debtors and the privileged few who are net creditors, a division that today may be more or equally relevant than the standard economic division between capitalists and laborers. That is, net debtors of all countries share— economically, culturally, and socially—more in common with net debtors of other countries than they share with net creditors of their own country (Di Muzio 2015).

As we mentioned in Chapter 1, while the word does not even appear in the index, Piketty's book is in many ways about "debt." For there to be a return on capital invested, there must be a corresponding return that constitutes someone or something's obligation to produce an amount greater than that invested. Whether the return is a loan payment, rent, or profit, like any debt, it must be in addition to and greater than the initial loan or capital input. Consequently, it should come as no surprise that inequality has surged along with surging debt levels, and that once we understand the role of interest on debt in our economy, we can see how debt is essentially a *structural* regressive tax because of the way money is presently issued.

As it is presently constituted, every economic transaction—whether the purchase of a commodity, a rent or mortgage payment, a meal at a restaurant, or payment for some service—must contain interest on someone or something's debt. Even a portion of income and indirect tax payments will go to service the interest on the public debt held by bondholders.[18] In other words, a portion of the price of virtually everything we buy and every tax we pay is interest on a loan through which money was injected into the economy. The question is, to whom is the interest portion of the price going? The German researcher Helmut Creutz answers thus:

> The share of interest contained in prices…when redistributed, do not benefit all households and least of all the weaker ones. The overwhelming part of it flows towards those who have the most interest bearing assets at their disposal. More precisely: the richer one is, this means, the more interest bearing tangible and monetary capital one possesses, the larger is the share that one gets from the pot of the interests collected. The biggest loss is borne relatively, however by those households that have no interest yielding assets, or at least, none worth mentioning. They only pay in without ever getting anything back. (2010: 4)

The extent to which the top 1 percent and 10 percent control interest-bearing (as well as dividend- and rent-bearing assets) is evident in Table 4.1, as are the total debt levels by wealth percentile. In brief,

Table 4.1 Total income generating assets and debts by percentile of wealth: 2010

Asset type	Top 1%	Next 9%	Bottom 90%
Stocks and mutual funds	48.8	42.5	8.6
Financial securities	64.4	29.5	6.1
Trusts	38.0	43.0	19.0
Business equity	61.4	30.5	8.1
Non-home real estate	35.5	43.6	20.9
Total assets for group	50.4	37.5	12.0
Total debt for group	5.9	21.6	72.5

Data from Wolff (2012, 2013).

*the top 1 percent own over 50 percent of the wealth-generating assets, but
have only 5.9 percent of the debt.*

Margrit Kennedy (2012), drawing on Creutz and research on
the German economy, writes that some 35–40 percent of everything
we buy goes to interest to bankers, financiers, and bondholders. As
Ellen Hodgson Brown (2013) notes, that helps explain how wealth
is systematically transferred from the majority to the minority at the
top of the income pyramid. The one very key consequence of debt as a
technology of power is that domination through the redistribution of
money to the already rich is mathematically encoded into the system.

Consequently, we have constructed a debt-based monetary system
divided into a society of net debtors and net creditors, with the latter
comprising, at most, 1–5 percent of the population. If we were to graph the
difference, we would get something like the distribution (as in Figure 4.9)
based on a 1985 study in Germany (Kennedy and Kennedy 1995: 26).

To further appreciate the role of interest in our economy, Figure 4.10
and Table A.1 show the amount of interest paid each year in the United

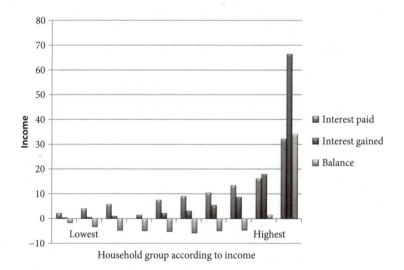

Figure 4.9 The distribution of net creditors and net debtors

Debt as Power

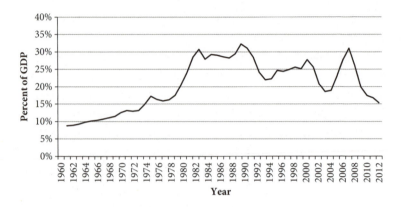

Figure 4.10 Interest paid as a percent of GDP

States from 1960 to 2012, and the percentage of the national income (GDP) that it represents.

Interest payments in 1960 amounted to some 46 billion dollars, or a little less than 9 percent of the national income. By 1982, interest payments amounted to over $1 trillion, or some 30 percent of the national income. The rapid rise in interest as a share of US national income was likely caused by the removal of the cap on interest rates, then about 6 percent, due, in turn, to the rise of inflation in the late 1970s and early 1980s that we discussed earlier. It may also be due, in part, to an increase in credit card use. Those caps, however, were never replaced, even when inflation rates declined to historically low levels. Since the early 1980s, the share of national wealth represented by interest has fluctuated between 15 and 31 percent, but since 1980, it has averaged a little over 25 percent of GDP. Essentially, this represents a tax on money, the tax going to private lenders, rather than to the public good.

To illustrate the extent of this transfer of wealth, consider that the amount of interest paid each year in the United States has, since 1978, exceeded the amount paid in federal taxes (Figure 4.11 and Table B.1).

In other words, US citizens pay more to private interests as the cost of issuing money than they pay to the Federal government in taxes to

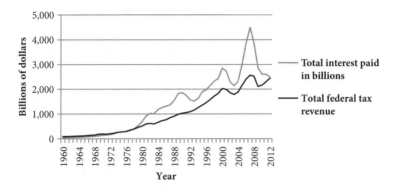

Figure 4.11 Total interest paid in the United States compared to total federal tax revenue, 1960–2012

Source: Office of Management and Budget, Historical Tables, Table 1.3; http://www.whitehouse.gov/omb/budget/Historicals/

run the country! If the United States had not assigned the right to create money to private interests, and had kept for itself the right to issue money as interest-bearing debt, it would have collected, in the period from 1960 to 2012, a sum equal to all Federal taxes with an additional $20 trillion left over for the public good.

Moreover, to the share of the national income siphoned off in interest on debt, we can add the cost of the financial industry in general, which Thomas Philippon (2014) calculates is at an all-time high of 9 percent of GDP. As Philippon (2014: 2) asks, "consider that 9 percent of US GDP last year was about $1.4 trillion—an unprecedented windfall for America's capitalist class. What does society get in return? Or, in other words, what does the finance industry produce?" This does not mean that we do not need a financial industry, as Philippon recognizes, whose role it is to produce, trade, and settle financial contracts, transfer resources, produce information, and provide incentives, to, as the 3rd Lord Rothschild put it, "facilitate the movement of money from point A, where it is, to point B, where it is needed" (Ferguson 2008: 63). The question is, when in earlier eras, as Philippon documents, such services could be provided at 2–4 percent of GDP, why now, with the great increase in communication technology, can't such services be provided far more inefficiently and cheaply?[19]

Our arguments in this book, also, should not be taken as an attack on the market, *per se*, however defined. There is nothing wrong with an economy in which people provide goods and services for others and receive an economic reward, even money, in return. However, the money that is used need not be created by a privileged few as interest-bearing debt through which they would accumulate a vastly disproportionate share of the society's wealth. In other words, while the market is a prerequisite for debt to be used as a technology of power, markets can function perfectly well without a money supply created by a private elite through debt, as the number of alternative currency arrangements around the world demonstrate (Hallsmith and Lietaer 2011). A perfectly workable modern market economy could be created if every individual received money only for productive work or, even, if every person, at the age of 18, was given a set amount with which to buy what was needed. This would not guarantee perfect equality, by any means, but it would ensure that people could choose what to do with their allocation and that, if they needed more, would offer goods or services that others demanded. It would not require perpetual, exponential growth and mounting dependence on a nonrenewable energy supply that destroys the biosphere.

Who controls the future?

Facing the impossibility of sustained exponential growth, mounting environmental problems, historically expensive oil, and wealth concentrating in ever fewer hands when levels of public, corporate, and consumer debts are expanding, the question becomes who, at this point in our history, controls the future?[20] If we were to project into the future, who would have the greatest say in what it will look like? No doubt this is a difficult question to answer, but without a sustained democratic movement against the use of debt as a technology of power, we anticipate that creditors, investors, and the giant firms they capitalize will continue to shape and reshape the limits of the possible for social reproduction and define the limits of how we address the problems we face. To illustrate this concern, we briefly mention the food and energy industries.

The future of food

One of the major long-term problems, particularly in the United States, is that of food supply; not that there is not enough, but, rather, too much. US food manufacturers produce some 3,900 calories a day per person. Their problem is selling it, which, if US obesity rates, particularly for children, are any indication, they are doing very effectively. The average American was some 23 pounds heavier in 2003 than their counterpart of 1960 and still getting heavier (Moss 2012; CDC 2013). This is such a worldwide trend that we could call the process the globalization of fatness and obesity (Roberts 2010; Raine 2012). It is not only about how many calories are consumed but also about the inequality of money and food options and the mass motorization of society that are chief contributors to the growing public health crisis.

There is also a problem with industrial agriculture; it is essentially unsustainable, dependent as it is on two rapidly diminishing resources— oil and water.[21] However, food production is a very profitable enterprise. But when we examine both US-style food production and consumption, we find an addiction to five things: oil and water on the production end, and salt, sugar, and fat on the consumption end. Our aim, here, is not to fully document the problem; that has been done extensively by others (e.g., Pollan 2007; Moss 2012; Gardner 2013). The question we want to ask is whether, under our present political economy, the global system of food production and consumption, which is hugely profitable, can be changed to one in which production is more sustainable and diets are healthier?

We may believe that we choose our food. But, clearly, what is available to us is controlled for the most part by large food companies who go to great lengths to discover our tastes and preferences. In a brilliant job of investigative reporting, Michael Moss (2013) describes how even when food companies try to do the "right thing" they are often stymied by investment capital.

In the early 2000s, there were executives at Kraft Foods genuinely alarmed at the contribution of the company to the obesity epidemic and were concerned about the consumer backlash and how it would affect the company in the long run. To get people to eat more of their product required manipulating the amount of sugar, fat, and salt in their foods, but it was resulting in negative health consequences. Could they promote healthier food and remain competitive in an industry that kept adding more sugar, salt, and fat?

At the time, Kraft was owned by Phillip Morris, and executives were worried that sugar, salt, and fat would bring down the processed food industry the same way as nicotine had brought down cigarettes. The tobacco industry, after years of fraud and denial, lost its big lawsuit brought by forty states whose health care programs were buckling under the pressures of tobacco-related illness. It cost the tobacco industry some $365 billion in the resulting lawsuits.

After years of carefully using just the proper amount of sugar, salt, and fat to maximize sales, Kraft made a decision to cap the amount of sugar, salt, and fat in their foods. However, the result was a drop in their stock price of some 17 percent at the same time as rivals were increasing at 5 percent. What ensued was a meeting with alarmed Wall Street analysts.

Moss describes a conversation a Kraft executive had with Wall Street analysts about lower-than-expected sales and the pressure to do something about it:

> "Do you think there's a bigger problem?" a Morgan Stanley analyst asked. "Because clearly you're underperforming your peers." "And what about all this talk about fighting obesity?," asked an analyst from Prudential Securities. "How was the company going to meet the projected sales growth of 3 percent if it was worrying about people's waistlines?" "You've obviously made a statement on obesity," the

analyst added. "But can you clarify the company's efforts in achieving a volume increase? You're going to try to grow your volume 2 to 3 percent domestically, it's almost got to make us fat." (Moss 2013: 257)

Under the pressure of investors and in competition with other food giants, Kraft's executives went back to fat, salt, and sugar and abandoned any attempt to make their products less harmful. More could be said about how the global food system is shaped and reshaped by the logic of differential capitalization and the need for corporate earnings. But this brief example highlights how one company's executives were more or less forced to maintain the excessive amounts of salt, sugar, and fat in their foods for the sake of earnings in the midst of an obesity epidemic in the United States and elsewhere.

The future of alternative energy

There are considerable debates over the future of energy. However, three main issues are relatively clear: (1) modern capitalism can be conceived of as a petro-market civilization since fossil fuels are the energy base that has allowed for the expansion and deepening of markets and the magnitude of monetary accumulation; (2) fossil fuels are nonrenewable and therefore this civilizational order is nonrenewable; and (3) the turn to coal, oil, and natural gas is altering the climate in ways that have impacted and will impact communities in harmful ways (Di Muzio 2012). Many recognize the need to transform our societies by finding alternative indicators of well-being and encouraging the switch to renewable energy and related technologies. However, studies also note that even if it were possible to run our societies on 100 percent renewable energy, what is not possible is the maintenance, let alone constant expansion of global growth into the next century (Trainer 2007; Heinberg 2011; Zehner 2012). Even if we were generous and included nuclear energy, renewables only make up 18.4 percent of global energy supplies—the remaining 81.6 percent consists of oil, natural gas, and coal. In other words, the transition to renewable energy will be protracted, and without significant direction and investment from public officials, it is unlikely to be accomplished. There are a number of important reasons for this but the one considered here is what matters most to creditors, investors, and capitalist firms: differential earnings and differential capitalization. Figure 4.12 compares the rise of capitalization in the oil and gas industry with that of its potential rival: the renewable energy industry. What the data demonstrate is that creditors and investors currently have little faith in the future profitability of the renewable energy industry relative its oil and gas counterpart.

Indeed, had you invested in the WilderHill index, you would have lost money from 2007 to 2012. However, had you invested in the oil and gas industry over the entire period, your investment would have grown by 182 percent. The reason is simple: the oil and gas industry is far more profitable than the renewable energy industry and capitalists chase differential returns not civilizational survival (Di Muzio 2012).

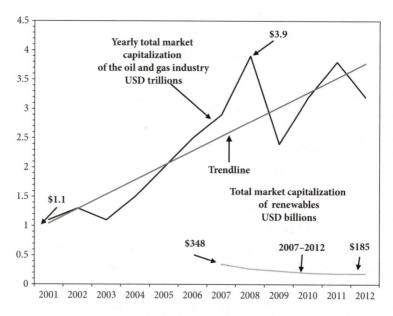

Figure 4.12 Comparison of capitalization of oil and gas and renewable energy

Sources: FT 500 2001–2012; WilderHill NEX

Until this goes into reverse or states make considerable investments in renewable energy, global society will be increasingly locked into an unsustainable petro-market world order that will go from crisis to crisis as oil becomes more expensive, debts mount, and austerity measures intensify.

Toward an expanding stark utopia?

When Karl Polanyi wrote *The Great Transformation*, he described the horrendous effects of the development and growth of the industrial economy: the dispossession of rural farmers from their land, widespread pauperization and misery, and the plundering of the natural world. Polanyi predicted that if left unchecked, the "free" market would create a "stark utopia" of human wretchedness and vast ecological damage. In the postwar years, he assumed that the Keynesian policies implemented during and after the Depression would provide such a check on industrial growth by the medium of democratic planning of the economy. But since Polanyi focused on the self-adjusting market as the "fount and matrix" of civilization rather than capitalist credit money, he could not fully foresee the price for maintaining a debt-based monetary system and the exponential economic growth that it requires. Nor could he propose a convincing alternative to the domestic and international monetary order. As suggested above, we are already bearing witness to a geography of stark utopias that stretch across many communities around the world. And the movement toward this stark utopia moves in increments so small that we hardly realize what is happening. We argue that to reverse and avoid its expansion, we need to confront possible alternatives that take money, the environment, and the impossibility of exponential growth seriously—the subject of our final chapter.

Solutions: A Party of the 99% and the Power of Debt

Money is one of the shatteringly simplifying ideas of all time, and like any other new and compelling idea, it creates its own revolution. (Bohannan 1959: 503)

There is an episode of the cartoon series South Park—*Margaritaville* (2009)[1]—addressing the financial crisis of 2007/08. In it, Kyle Broflovski, the only Jewish character in the series, risks death to save the community from economic disaster by transferring everyone's credit card debt to his own so they could resume buying stuff. The episode is a brilliant juxtaposition of economics and religion and highlights the many religious traditions in which redemption is achieved by freedom from all obligations, the freedom, as it were, from debt (Burridge 1969: 6–7). It is also a commentary on the 1887 book of the German philosopher Friedrich Wilhelm Nietzsche titled *On the Genealogy of Morals*. Commenting on the fact that the German word for "debt" (*schuld*) is also the word for "guilt" or "sin," Nietzsche speculates that in Christianity, God becomes the ultimate creditor of human indebtedness, and, of course, its ultimate forgiver by dying for its sins (see Ahn 2010; Graeber 2011: 76ff).

This idea that the debtor–creditor relationship is central to our sense of moral obligation, and that ultimate power can be conceptualized as the debtor–creditor relationship, puts the lie to the classical economic idea that money is neutral and simply a means of exchange, a unit of account and store of value. If you have the power to create money through the medium of interest-bearing debt, once you lend it into existence, you are replicating what, for Nietzsche, is the primal relationship of power and the source of morals and civilization itself.

As we have tried to show, the consequences of that experiment include continuing environmental devastation, growing social and economic inequality, and the continuing centralization of political power. Dozens of books and studies have carefully documented these developments (e.g., Reich 2012; Harvey 2014; Klein 2014; Piketty 2014; Robbins 2014; Di Muzio 2015), and most have concluded with recommendations for reform: for Piketty it is a tax on wealth to begin some form of redistribution and for Naomi Klein it is a grassroots movement; while Ellen Hodgson Brown (2014) advocates the growth of public banks, Bernard Laeiter suggests the development of alternative currencies, to name only a very few recommendations for reform. The dream, writes David Harvey (2010: 247), "would be a grand alliance of all the deprived and the dispossessed everywhere. The aim would be to control the organization, production and distribution of the surplus product for the long-term benefit of all."

While all are, to some extent, correct in their evaluations of the problems, and while all the recommendations would serve, if implemented, to reverse some of the negative externalities that result from a debt-based economy and the perpetual growth it requires, none offers a way to counter the power that capital represents. In this final chapter we want to offer, first, twelve solutions, most reflecting those proposed by others, that would become a political platform of a Party of the 99% (see Di Muzio 2015). We will then suggest the steps necessary to implement these proposals and a political strategy based on the idea that debt is a technology of power that can be utilized by debtors, as well as creditors.

The platform of the Party of the 99%

First, a Party of the 99% should be organized around the reform of its country's monetary system. We have tried to show that the present state of affairs began with a single act: the act of bestowing on private individuals the right and the power to issue interest-bearing money. Consequently, addressing the results of that act requires taking that right away. The current system of creating money through debt only benefits the owners of the banks. The rest of us, with insufficient incomes for what the economy can produce, get mounting debt that pushes up prices (inflation) and an economy that is effectively controlled by whether bankers feel confident to lend at profit (Rowbotham 1998: 292). The over $27 trillion in total interest on debt paid out in the United States from 2006 to 2013 represents the price US debtors pay for receiving money as interest-bearing debt, and was greater than the total GDP of all but two other countries in the world—China and Japan.

The goals of public banks include: (1) investments that create jobs in the local community, (2) investments that encourage the production of the most durable goods, (3) investments in research and development to enhance the quality of life, (4) investments in renewable energy, (5) investments in sustainable public infrastructure, and (6) investments in local sustainable agriculture.

Public banks are already common throughout the world. Ellen Hodgson Brown (2013), in her book *The Public Bank Solution: From Austerity to Prosperity*, points out that publically owned banks account for 40 percent of all banks globally, particularly in the BRIC countries: 45 percent of all banks in Brazil, 60 percent in Russia, 75 percent in India, and 69 percent or more in China. As these countries rise in economic power, have better public debt to GDP ratios, and funnel wealth back to public projects, it may be necessary for wealthy countries to encourage the development of public banking or nationalize existing banks in order to keep up. These countries have even formed a BRICS Development Bank to challenge the IMF and the World Bank (Chen 2014).

Second, we must eliminate Third World debt. Developing countries receive about $136 billion in aid from donor countries, including debt cancellations. But they pay out to rich countries in debt service about $600 billion, much of it in the compound interest of loans granted to deposed rulers (Hickel 2014). Estimates are that from 2002 to

2007 the net flow of money from poor to rich countries was minus $2.8 trillion (Abugre 2010).

As we pointed out previously, most of that debt reflects absurd conditions, rank incompetence, or a cynical abuse of power by lending agencies. Since debt repayment must be taken from national budgets for education, health care and poverty alleviation it is also of questionable morality. And, as the recent Ebola epidemic illustrated, the costs in devastated health systems are no longer confined to these countries. To add to this debt burden, developing countries lose about $1 trillion a year in capital flight, largely tax avoidance by multinational corporations.

Third, education, health care, and childcare should be universal and free. This will be easier to accomplish in some countries than in others, since many of the most civilized countries already provide nonprofit health care and education up to and including postsecondary education. This provision will mostly aid developing countries whose health and education budgets have been slashed through IMF structural adjustment programs. These services should be accessible to all and paid, debt-free, from the new public banking system and with funds saved through the canceling of odious debt. This will also contribute to bringing living standards of developing countries into line with that of the wealthy countries.

Fourth, a Party of the 99% should ban all private money from politics and those running for public office must be given a reasonable set of public funds to run their campaigns. A new political party should be eligible for reasonable start-up money as long as it meets certain criteria, such as a certain number of supporters. This will help eliminate fringe or less serious parties. Campaigns should be short in duration so money can be used for other priorities.

Fifth, a Party of the 99% should aim to abolish the wasteful and innovation-killing patent system. Patents were the original way in which a monarch granted a monopoly to private interests—typically for an invention. Some believe that patents are the only way to encourage innovation: they reason that "inventors" invent only if they can profit from their discovery. But this is ridiculous. Neoliberal economists like to argue that contributions from entrepreneurs such as Steve Jobs or Bill Gates or literary accomplishments, such as J.K. Rowling's Harry Potter series, would not have been possible without existing patent protection (Mankiw 2013). But the idea that Rowling would have written the Harry Potter books only if she knew that they would make her a billionaire and that Bill Gates expected to earn $80 billion from his efforts is absurd. The irony of such claims, of course, is that it is only by government regulation that such protections are forthcoming. And as Dean Baker (2013) points out, government could have easily cut the length of such monopolies in half, or return to the 14-year limit of the past instead of the present ninety-five-year limit in the United States.

And government-granted drug monopolies add hundreds of millions of dollars to health care costs, particularly in the United States and, worse, yet, push such drugs out of the reach of the poor who, given the forced reduction of public health budgets in the developing world, most need them (e.g., Baker 2005).

Hence the best solution is to abolish patents entirely through strong constitutional measures and to find other legislative instruments, less open to lobbying and rentseeking, to foster innovation whenever there is clear evidence that laissez-faire undersupplies it (Boldrin and Levine 2012).

Sixth, a Party of, by, and for the 99% should make insurance public and not for profit. Insurance works on the principle of the law of large numbers: the larger the number of people involved in the insurance scheme, the less likely it is that everyone will experience the same calamity. People who do suffer an injury or accidental death are paid out of the contributions provided by those who do not experience an accident or injury. There is no reason whatsoever why insurance provision should be owned by private individuals making money out of the misfortune of others. The absurdity of the present insurance system is evidenced by the practice of employers taking out life insurance policies on their employees, with the employer-companies as beneficiaries (Gelles 2014). Because company-owned life insurance confers generous tax benefits on employers, hundreds of corporations have taken out such policies on thousands of employees, while banks, such as JP Morgan and Chase, count billions of dollars on their books as evidence of their ability to withstand economic shocks.

Once again, the publicly run banking system can provide for this debt-free, with no premiums required. In other words, everyone is covered by virtue of being a member of the political community.

Seventh, a Party of the 99% should fund retirement at a democratically agreed-upon age. Presently, because of the economic insecurity wrought by the 2008 financial crisis and the defunding of pension plans by governments and municipalities bankrupted by debt, retirement is out of reach for many. Consequently, the elderly are forced to continue working longer (see Table 5.1).

While many may be working longer by choice, most continue working because savings, pensions, and social security are not enough. Moreover, the number of elderly working population is expected to increase further in the United States as baby boomers retire. A recent survey found that 62 percent of people aged 45–60 plan to delay retirement, up from 42 percent in 2010 (Brandon 2013).

In addition, by delaying retirement, jobs become less available for young people wishing to enter the workforce. Arguably one of the biggest problems in the developing world is the high unemployment

Table 5.1 Percentage employed of US men and women working full time by age group, 1995 and 2005

Age	Men			Women		
	1995	2005	% Change	1995	2005	% Change
55–61	91.8	91.8	0	74.6	78.7	6
62–64	77.9	81.2	4	58.9	65.8	12
65	65.4	73.7	13	45.9	56.8	24
66–69	52.3	65.7	26	34.8	49.5	42
70+	44.2	51.7	17	29.6	39.2	32

See Gendell (2006).

rate among the young. Over 70 million young people are out of work—12.6 percent—an increase of 3.5 million between 2007 and 2013 (ILO 2013).

Eighth, a Party of the 99% should provide each adult individual with a guaranteed income through the public bank. The income should be set at a level that secures a basic standard of living. A guaranteed standard of living produces important social goals by taking the power of the sack away from employers. First, it establishes a rule of greater freedom than is currently enjoyed by the majority of workers. The idea is premised on the fact that we are creative, productive beings and work is a large part of our subjectivity or identity. Most people want to work but they want to work in employments that are meaningful to them. With a secure income, we can be sure that those who work for added income will be doing so because they want to contribute to society in some way. Second, a guaranteed income solves the problem of unemployment and does not create any new debt. Third, with a guaranteed income, people will likely choose to work less, increasing their leisure time and potentially leading to a drop in the consumption of goods and services. This is a worthwhile goal not only because leisure time is valued by all but also because people will probably consume less. Without doubt, some will be up in arms about this proposal in such a materialistic economy, where social status is connected to possessions and shaped by advertising and marketing. But, from a sane point of view, we know from studies that after a certain threshold of wealth, individuals are no happier having more and more stuff. It seems that acquiring more and more possessions is not about happiness but about power and the demonstration of it. If we displace the logic of differential accumulation and stop creating debt money, no one will make enough money to acquire an inordinate amount of goods in the first place.

Ninth, a Party of the 99% should seek every way possible to transition away from fossil fuels and stem the growing threat of climate change. There are no quick fixes here, but time is of the essence if we want the transition to be relatively painless and peaceful. Three important studies have convincingly demonstrated that there is no way to socially reproduce current patterns of high energy consumption in rich countries with alternative energy (Trainer 2007; Heinberg 2009; Zehner 2012). Of course, a Party of the 99% should invest in renewable energy and implement renewable energy schemes wherever possible, but the Party should also have a program to reduce material consumption and promote low-energy leisure activities. As suggested, a guaranteed income should help in this pursuit.

Tenth, all parties of the 99% should work together to demilitarize the world. The military industry is also capitalized by dominant owners and they profit from conflict or the threat of conflict. Most of the bill is paid for by taxpayers and future generations, not to mention with the lives of soldiers and innocents. This is wasteful expenditure and we should not have our scientists working on solutions for how to kill people more effectively. In a social order where everyone is guaranteed a decent standard of living and there is no chance of gaining excessive power over others, there will be no need for a military. Some may recoil at this suggestion and believe it unrealistic, but the idea has deep roots in the liberal tradition. Concerned with the potential for a military dictatorship, people always feared standing armies. It was only with the rise of the capitalist mode of power that professional militaries became a cornerstone of Western states. As the capitalist mode of power withers, so too will the need for wasteful expenditure on an apparatus of violence, surveillance, and death.

Eleventh, a Party of the 99% should ensure that the only income stream available other than the guaranteed income from the public bank comes from a person's direct labor. What this means is that no one will be able to capitalize the labor power of another or take undeserved rewards. Individuals will be free to form producing associations, and, if they require investment, they can issue a proposal to the public bank. Provided that it meets the objectives of the public bank, the money can be created for the project. All projects funded by the bank should be transparent: this means that the entire entrepreneurial plan is made public. All businesses must be run on a not-for-profit basis and the 99% should design a salary schedule for each employment, with strict caps at the top. Should some jobs that are necessary for the reproduction of society fall into abeyance because no one wants to do them, the government can offer special inducements where these jobs are necessary to support a decent quality of life for all. It could very well be that those working in sanitation and health end up making the most money—but, of course, always within democratically decided reason.

Finally, promote other alternative financial systems, most notably those based on alternative or local currencies, that are designed to avoid interest, keep money circulating, and keep it in local communities (see, e.g., Kennedy 1995; Hallsmith and Lietaer 2011). One of the most successful of the thousands of local currencies existent today is Ithaca Hours, the alternative currency created by Paul Glover (1995) in Ithaca, New York, in the 1980s (see Papavasiliou 2008, 2010). Such local currencies are monetary alternatives to microcredit, which uses the mechanism of debt to affect social and economic change. Instead of microcredit, we need to promote the development of alternative currency systems that promote trade and exchange, rather than locking local economies into currency systems that promote debt and inhibit exchange. By promoting local trade, Papavasiliou (2010: 210–211) suggests, we create direct relationships between producers and consumers that protect local economies from "free trade" commodities and services that don't reflect the social and environmental costs of production and don't pit the benefit of cheaper prices against the long-term costs of deteriorating local economic and social conditions.

These twelve points are not a magical panacea for a perfect world free of all social ills and of the vast ecological problems we face. Nor, of course, are they the only steps necessary. For example, we also need to adopt a means of measuring societal well-being that replaces the GDP, such as the Genuine Progress Indicator (Costanza et al. 2009). We also need to address problems specific to some countries, such as student debt in the United States. But the suggested twelve points are close to a minimum of things that need to be done to repair the environment, reduce inequality, and inject greater accountability into global political systems.

Of course the immediate response to such proposals would be that these goals, while perhaps worthwhile, are completely unrealistic. As we noted earlier when Thomas Piketty proposed the simple expedient of a global wealth tax to stem the growing inequality of income and wealth, something as easy to implement theoretically as any land or income tax, he noted that even this, seemingly small measure, was unrealistic and "utopian." What hope then for the twelve points above?

We want to suggest that the above measures are at least worth debating and that a Party of the 99% has the means to promote change provided, first, that we correct the ideological imbalance that exists in the creditor–debtor relationship and that we implement a strategy based on the existence of debt as a technology of power.

The debtor as cultural hero

For debt to be maintained as a technology of power exercised by the 1% requires a financial, legal, and ideological structure that vastly privileges the creditor over the debtor. As Graeber points out, the creditor–debtor relationship is the central hierarchical relationship of our society. Debtors are contrasted with "savers," the thrifty ones that carefully plan for the future and never "spend beyond their means." We still hear that the financial crisis of 2008 was caused by people who bought 4,000-square-foot homes with loans that they couldn't afford or governments spending lavishly. As mentioned earlier, the dominant metaphor operative here is one of household finance; a family is spending more than it takes in. But that metaphor wholly misrepresents and obscures the nature or creation of debt in our economy.

First, it is almost impossible to function without personal debt in a global economy where money has been made purposefully scarce by the private power of the owners and managers of banks. A person's first loan is likely to be for education, as students need to borrow for higher education. While there is some debate regarding the degree of dependence of students on loans, presently student debt in the United States has surpassed one trillion dollars. Even if someone chooses not to attend college and get a job, she or he will likely have to borrow to purchase a car. Commercial lenders are so desperate to find profitable investments that there is a booming business in the United States in lending to the working poor—those with impaired credit—who need cars to get to work. Bundled into securities to be sold to investors, they grew at a rate of over 300 percent between 2010 and 2014 (Corkery and Silver-Greenberg 2015). These subprime auto loans pay up to 23 percent interest and are driving workers into bankruptcy (Silver-Greenberg and Corkery 2014).

Second, without debt, there would be no money. Money, in reality, represents the promise of borrowers to labor to repay it and the interest. Furthermore, as we noted, debts are created as assets by banks and financial institutions in the same way as factories produce automobiles. It is the creditor, after all, who creates the money and benefits from its reproduction.

Third, debt is a part of every economic transaction, and a portion of every tax payment goes to service the interest on the public debt, as a portion of the price of virtually everything someone buys contains interest on someone's loan. That means that almost everyone is a net debtor paying more in interest or dividends than they receive.

Finally, it is one thing for a friend to lend you some of her hard-earned cash. It is quite another to "borrow" money created out of thin air and feel some sort of moral obligation to repay it.

None of this is to imply that people shouldn't repay their debts. The problem is viewing them as moral obligations in a hierarchical relationship as opposed to a partnership. David Graeber (2013) summarized the mechanism for debt-shaming well: "The last thing the 1% wants, as the world economy continues to teeter from crisis, is to give up on one of their most powerful moral weapons: the idea that decent people always pay their debts."

To a great extent, the debt–creditor relationship is a perversion of the traditional partnership (as it is viewed in Islamic finance). One person is giving money to another and saying "make me more." But we do not treat it as a partnership; it is treated as a hierarchical relationship that makes the creditor far more powerful than the debtor.

Debt can exist only if the creditor has confidence that the income of the debtor will grow sufficiently to pay off the debt with interest as our whole economy must rest on the assumption that the economy will grow exponentially. Without that assumption, our present economy and our financial system makes no sense.

It is important, of course, that the 99% be kept unaware that they have considerable power. One way to think about this, we suggest, is to understand that the real power lies not with investors but with the collective on whom the capitalists depend to generate the return on capital. More specifically, the real power lies with the debtor, not the creditor. Without the debtor to generate the return on capital, there can be no creditor, and as we have shown, in our present system of money creation there must be few creditors and many debtors.

Why is it that people have a moral obligation to repay their debts, while banks do not have a moral obligation to extend credit, even when the money they lend is created by them and when the withholding of credit leads to individual suffering, as well as financial, social, and political chaos? How can people be said to have a moral obligation to repay their debts when corporations, multilateral institutions, and national or local governments can unilaterally cancel or reorder debt obligations or unilaterally cancel negotiated pension rights, or seize the savings of depositors to repay foreign creditors, as they have done? How can debtors have a moral obligation to repay debts, when at least thirty Republican members of the US House of Representatives and thirty-three US Republican Senators, attempting to force budget cuts, voted against the government repaying its debt obligations?[2]

Lending and investing require risk to justify a demand for a return on capital. If risk is nullified through the idea that debt entails a moral as well as a financial obligation, then there is no justification for interest and/or dividends. Yet government policies, particularly over the past two decades, have virtually eliminated all risk by having taxpayers "bail out" investors and financial institutions. Thus, creditors are protected from loss, leaving debtors to assume the burden. There is no morality in this.

People must accept debt to function in the current economic world because money has been made scarce. In effect, we have far more of an obligation to assume debt than we have an obligation to repay it, for without the assumption of debt, there would be no money, and therefore no economy.

Debt as a technology of power revisited

Besieging politicians with demands and demonstrations, even in countries that are nominally democratic, clearly is not as effective in determining legislation as the capital drowning them in dollars or their currency of choice. And anarchists do have a point when they refuse to make such demands because, they say, it legitimizes the state's power (Graeber 2009). In fact, politicians have little power; as we maintain, it is capital that has the power that they wield through the technology of debt. The job of the capitalist state is to make the world safe for capital, using the mantra that what is good for capital is good for the people. When Margaret Thatcher and Ronald Reagan claimed that they wanted to take government off the backs of the people, they meant off the back of capital. By weakening the regulations that had been instituted to ward off the stark utopia that Karl Polanyi warned of, dominant owners had a field day as the wealth of the 1% soared, while the well-being of everyone else declined. Modern corporations are at least honest when they admit that their responsibility is not to customers, employees, or the community in which they function; their responsibility is to shareholders.

But how do you appeal to capital? The genius of capitalist power is its invisibility and anonymity. The insidiousness of this power is that it has been normalized and naturalized, and therefore it largely goes unquestioned despite the serious consequences it has on people's everyday lives. If, as Jeffrey A. Winters (1996: x) suggested, unelected and democratically unaccountable creditors and investors were all to wear yellow suits and meet weekly in huge halls to decide where, when, and how much of their capital (money) to invest, there would be little mystery in their power. But, of course, they don't. Collectively they make private decisions on where, when, and how to distribute their investments. Furthermore, investors and creditors are free to do whatever they wish with their capital while states are virtually helpless to insist that private capital be used for anything other than what creditors and investors want to do with it.

The anonymity of creditors and investors and the structural power they hold present problems for political leaders: while the actions of creditors and investors can greatly influence our lives, it is political leaders that we often hold responsible for the rise and fall of a country's financial fortunes. So how might we think strategically about overcoming debt as a technology of power?

There is one way. Representatives of the 99% should communicate with capital when they service or pay off a debt. Household and individual bill-payers, along with business, corporate, and government accountants, constitute the channel of communication to capital. Each time a debt is serviced or paid, a portion, as we have seen, buttresses the power of capital and serves as a vote for the status quo. Each interest-bearing debt payment represents acquiescence to a system of money creation and distribution that sanctions the funneling of money and power to those that have the power to create money out of thin air. In a perfect world, those assigned that right would be working in the public interest and would be accountable to public needs. Massive demonstrations and violent actions may sometimes move capital, but generally the reactions are stopgap measures to defuse the protest. Besides, delegitimizing collective action and promoting a value system that emphasizes "individuality" and "freedom" defuses the potential for protest. Capital fares best when people shop and bowl alone.

The debt action and the implementation of debt as a technology of power

To understand how debt as power can be utilized to promote necessary change, we need to first recognize that the wealth of the 1% lies largely in the pockets of the 99% where it is supposed to work to produce interest and dividends. The power that the 99% retains *that has the potential to promote changes that, in the long run, benefit everyone is the right to withhold one's debt payments.* People are told, of course, that repayment of debt is a moral obligation; but debt, as outlined above, is not freely entered into. *As our economy is presently constituted, without debt, there would be no money.* Furthermore, if governments and municipalities can, without penalty, default on pension obligations or renounce obligations to protect children, the poor, and the elderly, surely we retain the right in the name of a just society to withhold our debt payments. By doing so, we deprive creditors, a small minority of our society, a source of their power and impel them to consider the harm that present arrangements inflict on all. *A debt strike must not constitute a refusal to pay debts*; rather it must be considered an act of civil disobedience to *withhold debt payments*, particularly on securitized debt (e.g., mortgages, automobiles, credit cards, and student loans), until action is taken to reform the presently unethical and unsustainable financial system. This would not be a strike against finance, per se; some means of managing the flow of capital is necessary. However, a financial system founded on debt and interest and the resulting need for perpetual growth is highly unethical and clearly unsustainable.

The idea of a debt action is hardly new; but generally the goals have been modest. There have been instances of national movements, such as El Barzón, an organization of debtors in Mexico, to resist foreclosures and repossessions due to debt default (Caffentzis 2013). There is also a movement in France to eliminate the public debt claiming that most sovereign debt is illegitimate (Keucheyan 2014). The organization, *Strike Debt!*, has set forth arguments for debt refusal (Ross 2014) focused on predatory behavior by the finance industry, and the organization *Rolling Jubille* was formed to raise funds for, as they put it, "A bailout of the people by the people."[3] We propose that a debt action have as a broader purpose the recognition that debt as a technology of power and the financial structure that it creates is at the root of most of our environmental, social, and political problems, and that unless it is addressed, there is little hope of solving them.

If a debt action, that is, the symbolic withholding of a month's payments by those concerned about climate change, corporate power, the decline of democracy, inequality, racial injustice, and colonial exploitation, is not doable, when it is legal and nonviolent and involves only a small financial penalty, then it is difficult to imagine any other way that the 99% could convey their concerns and instigate a movement for reform. Given the fact that it costs millions of dollars to successfully run for public office, asking politicians to take the message to finance is like asking someone to threaten the interests of their fabulously rich uncle who pays their allowance. Even people of faith must remember that the sole violent action of Jesus of Nazareth was his overturning of the money changer's tables in the Temple (Matthew 21:12), while the Koran has an outright ban on lending at interest—albeit circumvented in various ways.

Some might object to a debt action claiming that our economy and monetary system are built on trust. But we maintain that whatever trust existed has been severely violated by those in power, a violation evidenced by how they have used the power of debt to amass great wealth at the expense of everyone else. The purpose of the debt action is to hold capital accountable and to restore balance to our economic relationships.

The Party of the 99% with chapters around the globe can first announce its presence by declaring a debt holiday, a month set aside, say October 2016, during which securitized debts (home mortgages, student loans, car loans, and credit card loans) should go unpaid. This would involve a penalty, and additional profits for creditors, but it would be a small price to pay to publicize the presence and platform of the 99%.

The next step would be a debt action or strike. The mechanics of a debt strike are relatively easy to institute. As with the debt holiday, a date in the future should be set, at which point, unless there is significant movement to promote public banking and eliminate Third World debt, the first two items of our platform, citizens will withhold their debt payments until such actions are taken. Further debt actions can be instituted as needed. The effort must be global in scope. The requirement for perpetual growth is not one faced only by the wealthy countries of the world; it is faced by every country that has adopted a Western-style, debt-based financial system.

There will, naturally, be some concern on the part of debtors that their withholding of payments will result in some negative consequence (e.g., foreclosure or repossession of assets, fines, lowered credit rating). However, it will require only a small minority (e.g., some 20 percent) to begin the strike to make it impossible for creditors (or the government or financial institutions) to effectively impose penalties. Remember, creditors need debtors; they are the source of their power and discrediting a significant portion of them is not in their interest. Money, as Barbara Garson (2001) noted, has to keep working, and it is debtors who do most of the work. Thus, a debt strike will not be, as mentioned above, a refusal to pay debts, but rather an act of civil disobedience to effect change that will not only benefit all but save our economy from recurrent crises and collapse.

A debtor's strike is not without its dangers. If the strike succeeds and there is a refusal to implement reform, the economy will collapse in a credit crisis. A debt strike, in that regard, is no different than a labor strike; as in a labor strike, all parties have a vested interest in changing a situation that threatens the firm with collapse. However, without some form of financial reform, we remain a world in which ephemeral financial gain for the few can occur only by abandoning visions of free societies thriving in hospitable environments.

Appendix A

Table A.1 Interest paid and its percent of GDP in the United States from 1960 to 2012

Yearly range	Interest payments 1960–2012 (in billions)	GDP (in billions)	Interest paid as a percent of GDP
1960	46.1	526.4	8.76
1961	48.6	544.8	8.92
1962	54.4	585.7	9.29
1963	60.4	617.8	9.78
1964	67.2	663.6	10.13
1965	74.4	719.1	10.35
1966	84.1	787.7	10.68
1967	92.2	832.4	11.08
1968	104.6	909.8	11.50
1969	123.4	984.4	12.54
1970	141.8	1,075.9	13.18
1971	151	1,167.8	12.93
1972	168.6	1,282.4	13.15
1973	213.5	1,428.5	14.95
1974	267	1,548.8	17.24
1975	276.1	1,688.9	16.35
1976	298.2	1,877.6	15.88
1977	338.1	2,086	16.21
1978	412.8	2,356.6	17.52
1979	537.9	2,632.1	20.44
1980	687.8	2,862.5	24.03
1981	915.4	3,210.9	28.51
1982	1,028.1	3,345	30.74
1983	1,015.3	3,638.1	27.91

(*continued*)

Yearly range	Interest payments 1960–2012 (in billions)	GDP (in billions)	Interest paid as a percent of GDP
1984	1,181.9	4,040.7	29.25
1985	1,263.8	4,346.7	29.07
1986	1,313.1	4,590.1	28.61
1987	1,374.8	4,870.2	28.23
1988	1,546.9	5,252.6	29.45
1989	1,824.8	5,657.7	32.25
1990	1,858.1	5,979.6	31.07
1991	1,755.5	6,174	28.43
1992	1,578.6	6,539.3	24.14
1993	1,514.6	6,878.7	22.02
1994	1,628.2	7,308.7	22.28
1995	1,891.6	7,664	24.68
1996	1,976.9	8,100.2	24.41
1997	2,147.5	8,608.5	24.95
1998	2,328.4	9,089.1	25.62
1999	2,430.6	9,665.7	25.15
2000	2,856.5	10,289.7	27.76
2001	2,732.1	10,625.3	25.71
2002	2,284.4	10,980.2	20.80
2003	2,142	11,512.2	18.61
2004	2,324.6	12,277	18.93
2005	3,002.9	13,095.4	22.93
2006	3,852.8	13,857.9	27.80
2007	4,493.4	14,480.3	31.03
2008	3,848.3	14,720.3	26.14
2009	2,860	14,417.9	19.84
2010	2,609.4	14,958.3	17.44
2011	2,601.8	15,533.8	16.75
2012	2,498.6	16,244.6	15.38
2013	2,482.9	16,768.1	14.80

Source: EconoStats (http://www.econstats.com/nipa/nipa_3__1____y.htm).

Appendix B

Table B.1 Total interest paid compared to total federal taxes paid, 1960–2012 (in billions)

Year	Interest payments (in billions)	GDP	Interest paid as a percent of GDP (in billions)	Total US federal tax revenue	Total US federal tax revenue as a percent of GDP	Difference between interest paid and taxes paid
1960	46.1	526.4	8.76	92.5	17.57	46.4
1961	48.6	544.8	8.92	94.4	17.33	45.8
1962	54.4	585.7	9.29	99.7	17.02	45.3
1963	60.4	617.8	9.78	106.6	17.25	46.2
1964	67.2	663.6	10.13	112.6	16.97	45.4
1965	74.4	719.1	10.35	116.8	16.24	42.4
1966	84.1	787.7	10.68	130.8	16.61	46.7
1967	92.2	832.4	11.08	148.8	17.88	56.6
1968	104.6	909.8	11.50	153.0	16.82	48.4
1969	123.4	984.4	12.54	186.9	18.99	63.5
1970	141.8	1,075.9	13.18	192.8	17.92	51.0
1971	151	1,167.8	12.93	187.1	16.02	36.1
1972	168.6	1,282.4	13.15	207.3	16.17	38.7
1973	213.5	1,428.5	14.95	230.8	16.16	17.3
1974	267	1,548.8	17.24	263.2	16.99	−3.8
1975	276.1	1,688.9	16.35	279.1	16.53	3.0
1976	298.2	1,877.6	15.88	298.1	15.88	−0.1
1977	338.1	2,086	16.21	355.6	17.05	17.5
1978	412.8	2,356.6	17.52	399.6	16.96	−13.2
1979	537.9	2,632.1	20.44	463.3	17.60	−74.6
1980	687.8	2,862.5	24.03	517.1	18.06	−170.7

(continued)

Year	Interest payments (in billions)	GDP	Interest paid as a percent of GDP (in billions)	Total US federal tax revenue	Total US federal tax revenue as a percent of GDP	Difference between interest paid and taxes paid
1981	915.4	3,210.9	28.51	599.3	18.66	−316.1
1982	1,028.1	3,345	30.74	617.8	18.47	−410.3
1983	1,015.3	3,638.1	27.91	600.6	16.51	−414.7
1984	1,181.9	4,040.7	29.25	666.4	16.49	−515.5
1985	1,263.8	4,346.7	29.07	734.0	16.89	−529.8
1986	1,313.1	4,590.1	28.61	769.2	16.76	−543.9
1987	1,374.8	4,870.2	28.23	854.3	17.54	−520.5
1988	1,546.9	5,252.6	29.45	909.2	17.31	−637.7
1989	1,824.8	5,657.7	32.25	991.1	17.52	−833.7
1990	1,858.1	5,979.6	31.07	1,032.0	17.26	−826.1
1991	1,755.5	6,174	28.43	1,055.0	17.09	−700.5
1992	1,578.6	6,539.3	24.14	1,091.2	16.69	−487.4
1993	1,514.6	6,878.7	22.02	1,154.3	16.78	−360.3
1994	1,628.2	7,308.7	22.28	1,258.6	17.22	−369.6
1995	1,891.6	7,664	24.68	1,351.8	17.64	−539.8
1996	1,976.9	8,100.2	24.41	1,453.1	17.94	−523.8
1997	2,147.5	8,608.5	24.95	1,579.2	18.34	−568.3
1998	2,328.4	9,089.1	25.62	1,721.7	18.94	−606.7
1999	2,430.6	9,665.7	25.15	1,827.5	18.91	−603.1
2000	2,856.5	10,289.7	27.76	2,025.2	19.68	−831.3
2001	2,732.1	10,625.3	25.71	1,991.1	18.74	−741.0
2002	2,284.4	10,980.2	20.80	1,853.1	16.88	−431.3
2003	2,142	11,512.2	18.61	1,782.3	15.48	−359.7
2004	2,324.6	12,277	18.93	1,880.1	15.31	−444.5
2005	3,002.9	13,095.4	22.93	2,153.6	16.45	−849.3
2006	3,852.8	13,857.9	27.80	2,406.9	17.37	−1,445.9
2007	4,493.4	14,480.3	31.03	2,568.0	17.73	−1,925.4

(*continued*)

Year	Interest payments (in billions)	GDP	Interest paid as a percent of GDP (in billions)	Total US federal tax revenue	Total US federal tax revenue as a percent of GDP	Difference between interest paid and taxes paid
2008	3,848.3	14,720.3	26.14	2,524.0	17.15	−1,324.3
2009	2,860	14,417.9	19.84	2,105.0	14.60	−755.0
2010	2,609.4	14,958.3	17.44	2,162.7	14.46	−446.7
2011	2,601.8	15,533.8	16.75	2,303.5	14.83	−298.3
2012	2,498.6	16,244.6	15.38	2,450.2	15.08	−48.4
Total	$72,929.1		25.15	$53,108.1	17.06	

Source: Office of Management and Budget, Historical Tables, Table 1.3; http://www.whitehouse.gov/omb/budget/Historicals/ (last accessed April 21, 2014).

Notes

Chapter 1

1   Amy Waldman (2004) "Debts and Drought Drive India's Farmers to Despair," *New York Times*, June 6.

2   P. Sainath (2011) "In 16 Years, Farm Suicides Cross a Quarter Million," *The Hindu*, October 29.

3   The latter argues that India handled the 1991 crisis successfully, though the author may want to watch the documentary *Nero's Guests* to uncover how unequal the "success" was shared.

4   The transaction is also facilitated by the Buddhist religious-cultural belief that women are inferior to men and that all children owe a debt to their parents just for being born—a debt that children are obliged to repay. See Bales (2012).

5   BBC (2013) "The Bangladesh Poor Selling Organs to Pay Debts," October 28. http://www.bbc.com/news/world-asia-24128096 (June 13, 2014).

6   C. Cryn Johannsen (2012) "The Ones We've Lost: The Student Loan Debt Suicides," *Huffington Post*, February 7.

7   Editorial Board (2014) "Student Borrowers and the Economy," *New York Times*, June 10. As far as we know, the concept of "debtocracy" was introduced by Katerina Kitidi and Aris Hatzistefanou in their documentary of the same name on the economic crisis in Greece.

8   If we consider equities or shares in publically listed corporations as a form of debt, that figure would be closer to $242 trillion. Data on equity market capitalization are taken from the World Federation of Exchanges as of May 2014. http://www.world-exchanges.org/statistics/time-series/market-capitalization (June 9, 2014).

9   Market capitalization is the value of one share multiplied by the existing number of shares. For example, the US bank Wells Fargo & Co. has 5.27 billion shares outstanding and the value of one share at the time of this writing was $51.98, giving the firm a market capitalization of about $274 billion. Firms with the largest market capitalization typically have considerable power to shape and reshape social reproduction. There is

also a forward-looking element to market capitalization since investors capitalize *expected future* earnings.

10 http://www.imf.org/external/pubs/ft/survey/so/2014/res052314a.htm (June 8, 2014).

11 Credit Suisse's Research Institute estimates that the richest 10 percent of adults own 86 percent of all global wealth, with the top 1 percent accounting for 46 percent of it, while Oxfam (2015) estimates it is now over 50 percent. The bottom 3.2 billion of the population collectively own a mere 3 percent of global wealth (Credit Suisse 2013: 22). This suggests that the vast majority of humanity do not own any significant amount of shares in banking corporations. What privilege workers likely own in the pension or mutual fund schemes is likely negligible in comparison to the dominant owners.

12 Hembruff (2013) also argues that Graeber lacks a convincing theory of the state.

13 Hudson ([1972] 2003), Ingham (1999; 2004), Brown (2007), Mellor (2010), and Rowbotham (1998) certainly recognize the power dimensions of money creation but none of them theorize this as the *capitalized* power of a private minority of owners. A focus on capitalization as the key ritual of capitalist (money) accumulation is associated with the seminal work of Nitzan and Bichler (2009). Nitzan and Bichler do not, however, theorize the creation of money as debt. For a summary and engagement with their work, see Di Muzio 2014.

14 Polanyi writes, "The transformation to this system [capitalist market economy] from the earlier economy is so complete that it resembles more the metamorphosis of the caterpillar than any alteration that can be expressed in terms of continuous growth and development" ([1944] 1957: 42).

15 Douthwaite (in Heinberg 2010: 279–283) and Hall and Klitgaard (2012) notice the interconnections between energy and money, but their treatments are considerably undertheorized and require more empirical detail. See also, Di Muzio (2015).

16 In fairness to Graeber and his anarchist approach, any solution that involves action through government is no solution at all, since it legitimizes the very institutions seen as the root of the problem (see Graeber 2009: 203).

17   The term "nonindustrious poor" seems to be an oxymoron. Most poor
     people, by definition, have to be very industrious, though in ways
     Graeber may have overlooked.

Chapter 2

1   By rational pursuits, we do not imply "rational choice" theories that
     theorize humans as little more than calculative rational actors seeking
     to maximize pleasure and minimize pain in some abstract space absent
     history, politics, and power. Rather, we follow Foucault and argue that
     there are different rationalities for social action. But what unites them
     is the notion that they all involve reasons or justifications for action.
     This makes rationalities difficult to assess in any objective way. As such,
     we are left to critique and scrutinize the effects of these rationalities by
     subjecting them to ethical and democratic tests of legitimacy. Put simply,
     we judge their effects on social relations and the natural world.

2   Discounting is the process of evaluating the present value of a future
     payment or stream of income. For example, I may have a government
     bond that says that in 15 years' time, the government owes me $100. If I
     need the money now or don't trust that the government will repay, I may
     sell it on to another party. The other party will likely discount the bond,
     that is, pay less money for the $100 dollar bond. She may only pay me
     $90, but since I need the money now or do not trust that the government
     will repay me in the future, I would be happy to at least get $90 rather
     than some lesser amount in the future. Discounting is central to finance
     and is premised on the time value theory of money. This theory basically
     states that a dollar is worth more today than it is in the future because
     the dollar you have today can immediately start earning interest. The rate
     of interest is absolutely integral to capitalism, and without it, capitalists
     would have a difficult time assessing a normal rate of return and the
     future.

3   The oldest recognized exchange was established by the Dutch East India
     Company in 1602.

4   Data are from the World Federation of Exchanges: http://www.world
     -exchanges.org/about-wfe (accessed July 11, 2014).

5   The FT Global 500 are available for download at http://www.ft.com/intl/
     cms/s/0/988051be-fdee-11e3-bd0e-00144feab7de.html#axzz3O3vRstzX.

6   United States Federal Reserve. Z.1. *Financial Accounts of the United
     States*, http://www.federalreserve.gov/releases/z1/current/z1.pdf
     (accessed February 21, 2014). Figure as of June 5, 2014.

7   Martin Wolf (2014) "Strip Private Banks of Their Power to Create
     Money," *Financial Times*, April 24 and David Graeber (2014) "The Truth
     Is Out: Money Is Just an IOU and the Banks Are Rolling in It," *The
     Guardian*, March 18. *97% Owned* is also a telling documentary.

8   The general idea here is that the interest banks pay to depositors is always
     less than the interest they charge borrowers.

9   See also, David Pilling (2014) "Has GDP Outgrown Its Use," *Financial
     Times*, July 4.

10   *The Economist*, "Household Debt," June 1, 2013: http://www.economist
     .com/news/economic-and-financial-indicators/21578669-household-debt
     (accessed July 14, 2014).

11   As Brown has noted, "the elimination of a public debt by a central
     government is a rare happening in fiscal history" (1989: 4).

12   But to recall, since banks do not create interest when they contract loans,
     there is always more debt in the system than the ability to repay.

13   Piketty (2014: 206) notes, "In both France and Britain, from the
     eighteenth century to the twenty-first, the pure return on capital has
     oscillated around a central value of 4–5 percent a year, generally in an
     interval from 3–6 percent a year."

Chapter 3

1   Killingray notes that taxation and the emergence and growth of colonial
     policing were intimately intertwined.

2   The Maria Theresa thaler or dollar is a silver coin that originated in Austria
     but was minted elsewhere and widely circulated as a global trade currency.
     It was popular in many parts of Africa and the Middle East (Tschoegl 2001).
     Manillas are silver bracelets, while cowries are a particular type of sea shell.

3   As Kindleberger reminds us, borrowing for such endeavors was not
     exclusive to India. Royalty in Europe borrowed for "coronations,
     marriages and funerals" as well as war (1996: 29).

4   For example, in early modern England, estate records demonstrate that thousands of peasants were forced to flee the land due to unrepayable debts (Clay 1984: 90–95, 150). As the aristocracy and gentry borrowed to reinforce their social status, they too fell into unrepayable debt and were forced to sell some or all of their holdings in land. Debt and dispossession should be understood as concurrent practices, intimately intertwined and historically repeated in different times and places, with only the agents changing slightly.

5   http://www.economist.com/content/global_debt_clock (accessed January 18, 2014).

6   These events are a forerunner to the twentieth-century debates on declining terms of trade and the possibility of independent development, particularly in Latin America.

7   Political theory of the time has it that republics were best safeguarded when they were smaller territorial units.

8   A further reason for the proclamation was that it was easier to govern the population on the seaboard rather than inland.

9   Before the arrival of synthetic fertilizers, the growth of tobacco was extremely ruinous to the soil. Fertility was lost in four to five years, making it a necessity for owners of tobacco plantations like Jefferson and Washington to constantly seek out new lands westward.

10   The letters of Thomas Jefferson, 1743–1826. Letter to William Henry Harrison, 1803: http://www.let.rug.nl/usa/presidents/thomas-jefferson/letters-of-thomas-jefferson/jefl151.php (accessed August 24, 2014).

11   Much of the same still occurs today in the capitalist heartland. For instance, vulture capitalist firms are capitalized on the basis of collecting the bad debts of individuals (or nations) by purchasing them at a discount from their original issuers, as we will examine further in Chapter 4 (see Roberts in Gill and Cutler 2014: 243).

12   By 1787, Massachusetts applied heavy direct taxes in order to help repay its war debt and the share it owed to creditors of the Continental Congress. Debt had to be repaid in scare specie or its equivalent, forcing many into debtor's prison or to foreclose on their homesteads (Hammond 2003: 187–188).

13   New and cutting-edge empirical research by Sandy Hager on the United States has demonstrated that "the public debt has come to serve as an

institution of power working in the interests of the top one percent" (2013: 177). Over the past three decades, Hager's study found that the public debt effectively works as a mechanisms for redistributing income from the working class to wealthy bondholders of the 1 percent.

14 In one of his many letters on the subject to the *New York Tribune*, Marx spelled out what this transfer meant for Indian debt:

> The proprietors of East India stocks were to be paid out of the revenues enjoyed by the East India Company in its governmental capacity, and, by act of Parliament, the Indian stock, amounting to £6,000,000 sterling, bearing ten percent interest, was converted into a capital not to be liquidated except at the rate of £200 for every £100 of stock. In other words, the original East India stock of £6,000,000 sterling was converted into a capital of £12,000,000 sterling, bearing five percent interest, and chargeable upon the revenue derived from the taxes of the Indian people. The debt of the East India Company was thus, by a Parliamentary sleight of hand, changed into a debt of the Indian people.

> https://www.marxists.org/archive/marx/works/1858/02/09.htm (accessed August 27, 2014).

15 Jon Henly (2010) "Haiti's Decent into Hell," *Guardian UK*, January 14. Henly cites the British historian Alex Von Tunzelmann, whose quote is cited here.

16 The experience of China is far from the exception and rather demonstrates the rule.

17 UN Decolonization, http://www.un.org/en/decolonization/nonselfgov .shtml (accessed August 28, 2014).

18 The first president of Tanzania, Julius Nyerere, wrote that "The Third World is now blamed for its own poverty. Each country is analyzed separately by international institutions and by political commentators. Its problems are then explained in terms of its socialism, its corruption, the laziness of its people and such-like alleged national attributes. *The fact that virtually all Third World countries and certainly all the poorest of them, are in the same plight is largely ignored*" (1985: 489, our emphasis).

19 Morgan, Oliver and Faisal Islam (2001) "Saudi Dove in the Oil Slick," *The Observer*, January 14: http://www.guardian.co.uk/business/2001/jan/14/

globalrecession.oilandpetrol (accessed August 31, 2014). During an
interview with Morgan and Islam, the former Saudi oil minister Sheikh
Ahmed Zaki Yamani stated, "I am 100 percent sure that the Americans
were behind the increase in the price of oil. The oil companies were in
in real trouble at that time, they had borrowed a lot of money and they
needed a high oil price to save them." Presumably the oil companies
needed a high price for oil to repay their own debts to their bankers
and finance the North Sea development as well as Prudhoe Bay—both
relatively inhospitable territories posing significant challenges for oil
production.

20   On the connection between oil prices and recessions, see Hamilton (2009).

21   During the massive spike in oil prices from 2001 to 2008 when WTI
went as high as $134, the consumer price index remained relatively stable
in both the United Kingdom and the United States—the opposite of
what one might expect. The likely reason for this is the fact that wages
have been making up less and less of a percentage share of GDP since
de-unionization and the offshoring of production to parts of Central and
South America as well as Asia.

22   The claim that interest rates were also increased to attract foreign capital
is also untenable. The United States had already made a deal with the
Saudis for recycling petrodollars and other OPEC nations followed suit;
oil and other commodities were priced in US dollars and the United
States had the largest securities market on the planet. Moreover, investors
and countries held dollars in the United States when it went off gold
and they would have held them in the 1980s without diabolical interest
rates. The evidence is the fact that at record low interest rates today,
the United States has still not experienced a great "dump" of dollars as
some financial analysts have anticipated. See, "Still No Alternative to the
Dollar" *Financial Times*, video: http://video.ft.com/3592100572001/Still
-no-alternative-to-dollar/Markets (accessed August 31, 2014). Hudson
calls this phenomenon "monetary imperialism" ([1972] 2003: 385).

23   To recall, this debt was never to be paid off in full.

24   This is not to suggest that ideas are unimportant—far from—but to
see to it that ideas operate at a broad societal level; that is, to effect the
processes of social reproduction writ large, they must be connected up
with interests backed by institutional rule and technologies of power—
with debt as the leading weapon.

Chapter 4

1   In 1991 the GNP was turned into the GDP. With GNP, the earnings
    of a multinational firm were attributed to the country in which the
    firm was owned and where most of the profits would eventually
    return. With the change to GDP, however, the profits are attributed
    to the country where the factories or mines or other corporate assets
    are located, even though most of the profits won't stay there. Thus,
    GDP excludes overseas profits earned by US firms but includes profits
    earned in the United States by foreign firms. Although it makes little
    difference in the index of economic growth in wealthy countries,
    this accounting shift does raise the measure of economic growth in
    the poor or peripheral countries. However, it tends to hide the fact
    that profits extracted from the periphery are generally going to core
    countries.

2   But since, in a market society, all desired goods and services are available
    largely only to people with money, his argument is akin to saying that
    people who have access to food are healthier. And, of course, it enables
    them to repay their debts.

3   The computation is far from neutral and a very poor indicator of social
    well-being.

4   More recently, neoliberals are claiming that continued growth will help
    solve our environmental problems. They cite research that suggests
    that while countries in the initial stages of economic growth may
    experience increased environmental degradation, once per capita
    income reaches a certain point, the environment improves (see, e.g.,
    Chua 1999). They argue that since economic prosperity provides
    people with more money, citizens can use that money to create a
    demand for a cleaner environment. The problem with that claim is
    that, even if the research is useful—and there is much evidence that it
    is not (see, e.g., Harbaugh et al. 2002)—estimates of per capita income
    at which the environment improves range from $4,000 to $13,000.
    Since more than half the world's population earns $5,000 per capita
    or far less, billions must try to survive in increasingly devastated
    environments.

5   In the United Nations World Economic Survey for 1959 the authors note
    that

Increasingly it has become apparent that the realization of the goal of economic growth may render manageable the dominant economic problems, both national and international, which in a stationary economy might produce only conflict and frustration. (quoted in Arndt 1978: 62)

We should note that the neoliberal cannot ask why the economy must grow. This is the reason, perhaps, that major textbooks on economic growth (see, e.g., Jones 2002; Barro and Sala-i-Martin 2004; Aghion and Durlauf 2005) nowhere address that question.

6   We realize we have not dealt with the issue of population growth, which many assume to be the cause of the need for perpetual growth, and which many developmental theorists assume to be the cause of poverty, going back to Malthus (see Victor 2008). But economies must continue to grow at the minimum rate of 3–5 percent to avoid economic collapse, regardless of their rate of population growth, while the economies of most developed countries grew at high rates even when their populations were dramatically expanding (see Robbins 2014, Chapter 5 for a fuller discussion of this issue).

7   Milton Friedman put the minimum required growth at 5 percent per year.

8   It is difficult to conceptualize what these huge numbers mean and what the difference is between millions, billions, and trillions. To illustrate, if in the year 0, you had a trillion dollars (10^{12} or 10E12 in US scientific notation or a thousand billion) to spend, and you spent it at the rate of one million dollars (10^6 or 10E6) a day, you would spend a billion (10^{12} or 10E12) within 3 years, but, by 2010, you would have had 700 years remaining to spend the trillion. A quadrillion is 10^{15th} (or 10E15). At one million dollars a day, it would take 2.74 million years to spend a quadrillion. Even if you spent at the rate of a million dollars a second, it would still take almost 32 years to spend a quadrillion. Even if the US economy grew only at the average rate since 1870 (1.8 percent), by 2100, it would be 75 trillion (5 times what it is today) and the global economy would be 300 trillion, or more than 4 times what it is today.

9   We might even suggest that the guiding formula of our political economy is that of the exponential curve, $X_t = X_0(1+r)^t$.

10 Julien-François Gerber (2014: 13ff) notes how in early capitalism debt served to accelerate production to match the time period in which the debt had to be repaid. Gerber recognizes this as a general feature of capitalism.

11 To put that into some perspective, banks recommend that the price of a home should not exceed 250 percent of the borrower's yearly salary. Of course, that loan mortgage would not be granted unless the borrower had a credit rating that ensured that there was an excellent chance of loan repayment. And, of course, the bank has a lien on the home until the debt is repaid.

12 Prior to 1989, coffee prices were regulated by the International Coffee Organization. Initiated with support of coffee-producing and coffee-importing countries, the organization formed to address the fall in coffee prices in the 1950s. The system worked to afford producers at least a small profit until 1989, when quota limits were eliminated due largely to the efforts of the United States, following which coffee prices plunged (Tucker 2011: 121).

13 As of April 2015, the issue of debt payment for Argentina is unresolved, as negotiations continue between Argentina and its creditors, while the right of a US judge to issue a judgment itself is being questioned.

14 http://data.worldbank.org/indicator/NY.GDP.MKTP.CD (accessed September 27, 2014).

15 The buying of bad debt is a practice that traces back prior to the Civil War in the United States. Abraham Lincoln, in fact, signed a promissory note when he bought a general store from a man named Reuben Radford but was unable to pay. Radford sold the note to the debt buyer, Peter Van Bergen. Van Bergen then successfully sued Lincoln, whose tools and saddle were seized and auctioned off to pay the debt (Halpern 2014: 21–22).

16 The Federal Reserve Bank of the United States is the only central bank among developed countries with the dual role of controlling inflation *and* maintaining employment. In practice, it generally places a far greater priority on the former and virtually none on the latter. By keeping inflation low, it ensures that banks and other lenders are repaid in money whose value is close to that lent. But it also limits the growth of the

economy by limiting economic activity, and, hence, limiting job creation. It has long been a policy of central banks to increase interest costs when unemployment rates fall below 5 percent.

17 The 1% claim that they are the job creators, although as Robert Reich (2012) points out, it is consumers and laborers that make the greater contribution. Clearly, only if people have resources to spend and employment to earn money can the economy grow and debt be repaid.

18 But we note that the government does not have to wait around for tax receipts to spend money into the economy. In the United States, the federal government simply spends from its account at the Federal Reserve. For a detailed account of this process, see Bell (2000).

19 To the share of GDP taken by finance in interest, fees, expenses, and so on, we can also add the additional amount taken from taxpayers to bailout banks and other financial institutions after the latest crash, which, so far, amounts to some $53 billion (ProPublica 2015), to which we could also add the sum of $900 billion in tax dollars, or $32 billion a year, as the ultimate cost to taxpayers of the savings and loan crisis of the late 1980s (Zepezauer and Naiman 1996).

20 In the United States, there is, in fact, substantial research that shows that in policy-making and legislation, the 1% have far more influence than the 99%. The most recent study by Martin Gilens and Benjamin Page (2014) demonstrates that ordinary US citizens have virtually no influence over policy (see also Kaiser 2010; Kuhner 2014).

21 http://www.un.org/waterforlifedecade/scarcity.shtml (accessed February 1, 2015).

Chapter 5

1 "Margaritaville" won the 2009 Emmy Award for Outstanding Animated Program for Programming Less Than One Hour and was released along with the rest of the thirteenth season on March 16, 2010.

2 See http://www.senate.gov/legislative/LIS/roll_call_lists/roll_call _vote_cfm.cfm?congress=113&session=1&vote=00011; http://projects .washingtonpost.com/congress/113/house/1/votes/30/.

3 See rollingjubilee.org.

Bibliography

Abu-Lughod, Janet L. (1989) *Before European Hegemony: The World System, AD 1250–1350* (Oxford: Oxford University Press).

Aburge, Charles (2010) "Development Aid: Robbing the Poor to Feed the Rich," *Pambazuka News*. Issue 485. http://pambazuka.org/en/category/features/65096

Aghion, Philippe and Steven, Durlauf (2005) *Handbook of Economic Growth I* (Amsterdam: Elsevier).

Ahn, Ilsup (2010) "The Genealogy of Debt and the Phenomenology of Forgiveness: Nietzsche, Marion, and Derrida on the Meaning of the Peculiar Phenomenon," *Heythrop Journal*, Vol. 51, No. 3: 454–470.

Andreou, Alex (2013) "If You Think You Know What 'Debt' Is, Read on," *The Guardian*, July 29.

Anghie, Antony (2005) *Imperialism, Sovereignty and the Making of International Law* (Cambridge: Cambridge University Press).

Annisette, M. and D. Neu (2004) "Accounting and Empire: An Introduction," *Critical Perspectives on Accounting*, Vol. 15: 1–4.

Aoyama, Kaoru (2009) *Thai Migrant Sex Workers: From Modernization to Globalization* (Basingstoke: Palgrave MacMillan).

Arndt, H. W. (1978) *The Rise and Fall of Economic Growth: A Study in Contemporary Thought* (Chicago: University of Chicago Press).

Arrighi, Giovanni (1994) *The Long Twentieth Century* (New York: Verso).

—— (2007) *Adam Smith in Beijing: Lineages of the Twenty-First Century* (London: Verso).

Baker, Dean (July, 2005) "The Reform of Intellectual Property," *Post-Autistic Economic Review*, Number 32. http://www.paecon.net/PAEReview/issue32/Baker32.htm

—— (2013) *The Bigger Problem with Mankiw's Plan to Give Everything to the One Percent* (Center for Economic and Policy Research). http://www.cepr.net/index.php/blogs/beat-the-press/the-bigger-problem-with-mankiws-plan-to-give-everything-to-the-one-percent

Bakker, Isabella and Stephen Gill (eds) (2003) *Power, Production and Social Reproduction* (Basingstoke: Palgrave MacMillan).

Bales, Kevin (2012) *Disposable People: New Slavery in the Global Economy* (Berkeley: University of California Press).

Banner, Stuart (2005) *How the Indians Lost Their Land: Law and Power on the Frontier* (Cambridge, MA: Belknap Press).

Bannerjee, Prathama (2000) "Debt, Time and Extravagance: Money and the Making of 'Primitives' in Colonial Bengal," *Indian Economic Social History Review*, Vol. 37: 423–445.

Barro, Robert J. (1998) *The Determinants of Economic Growth* (Cambridge: MIT Press).

Barro, Robert J. and Xavier Sala-i-Martin (2004) *Economic Growth* (Second Edition) (Cambridge: The MIT Press).

Baskin, Jonathan Barron and Paul J. Miranti Jr. (1997) *A History of Corporate Finance* (Cambridge: Cambridge University Press).

Bauman, Zygmunt (2004) *Wasted Lives: Modernity and Its Outcasts* (Cambridge: Polity Press).

Beard, Charles A. ([1913] 1962) *An Economic Interpretation of the Constitution of the United States* (New York: The Macmillan Company).

Beatty, Jack (2007) *The Age of Betrayal. The Triumph of Money in America, 1865–1900* (New York: Alfred A. Knopf).

Bell, Stephanie (2000) "Do Taxes and Bonds Finance Government Spending?," *Journal of Economic Issues*, Vol. 34, No. 3: 603–620.

Bhambra, Gurminder K. (2007) *Rethinking Modernity: Postcolonialism and the Sociological Imagination* (Basingstoke: Palgrave MacMillan).

—— (2010) "Historical Sociology, International Relations and Connected Histories," *Cambridge Review of International Affairs*, Vol. 23, No. 1: 127–143.

Blackburn, Robin (2010) *The Making of New World Slavery: From the Baroque to the Modern, 1492–1800* (London: Verso).

Blanc, Jérôme (ed.) (2012) "Thirty Years of Community and Complementary Currencies: A Review of Impacts, Potential and Challenges," *International Journal of Community Currency Research*, Vol. 16, Special issue.

Blum, William (2004) *Killing Hope: CIA and US Military Interventions since World War II* (London: Zed Press).

Boak, Josh (2014) "Americans in Debt: 35 Percent Have Bills Reported to Collection Agencies," *Huffington Post*, July 29. http://www.huffingtonpost .com/2014/07/29/americans-in-debt_n_5629137.html

Bogin, Ruth (1989) "'Measures so Glaringly Unjust': A Response to Hamilton's Funding Plan by William Manning," *The William and Mary Quarterly*, Vol. 46, No. 2: 315–331.

Bohannan, Paul (1959) "The Impact of Money on an African Subsistence Economy," *The Journal of Economic History*, Vol. 19, No. 4: 491–503.

Boldrin, Michele and David Levine (2012) *The Case against Patents*. Working Paper 2012-035A. Federal Reserve Bank of St. Louis. http://research .stlouisfed.org/wp/2012/2012-035.pdf

Bond, Patrick (2003) *Against Global Apartheid: South Africa Meets the World Bank, IMF and International Finance* (London: Zed Books).

Bonilla, Stephania (2011) *Odious Debt: Law and Economic Perspectives*. PhD Thesis (Hamburg: Gabler).

Bonner, William and Addison Wiggin (2009) *The New Empire of Debt* (Hoboken: John Wiley & Sons Inc.).

Bouton, Terry (2001) "Review: Whose Original Intent? Expanding the Concept of the Founders," *Law and History Review*, Vol. 19, No. 3: 661–671.

Bracking, Sarah (2009) *Money and Power: Great Predators in the Political Economy of Development* (London: Pluto Press).

Bradbury, Katherine (2011) *Trends in U.S. Family Income Mobility, 1969–2006*. Working Paper # No. 11–10. Federal Reserve Bank of Boston. http://www .bostonfed.org/economic/wp/wp2011/wp1110.pdf

Braddick, Michael J. (1996) *The Nerves of State: Taxation and the Financing of the English State, 1558–1714* (Manchester: Manchester University Press).

Brandon, Emily (2013) 'Why More Americans Are Working Past Age 65," *U.S. News and World Report*, February 11. http://money.usnews.com/ money/retirement/articles/2013/02/11/why-more-americans-are-working- past-age-65

Braudel, Fernand (1985) *Civilization and Capitalism, 15th to 18th Century*. Three Volumes (Berkeley: University of California Press).

Breen, T. H. (1985) *Tobacco Culture: The Mentality of the Great Tidewater Planters on the Eve of Revolution* (Princeton: Princeton University Press).

Brenner, Robert (July–August, 1977) "The *Origins of Capitalist Development*: A Critique of Neo-Smithian Marxism," *New Left Review*, Vol. I, No. 104: 25–92.

––––– (2002) *The Boom and the Bubble: The US in the World Economy* (London: Verso).

Brewer, John (1989) *The Sinews of Power: War, Money and the English State: 1688–1783* (London: Unwin Hyman).

Brown, E. Cary (1989) *Episodes in the Public Debt History of the United States.* Working Paper No. 540. Department of Economics, MIT.

Brown, Ellen Hodgson (2007) *The Web of Debt: The Shocking Truth about Our Money System and How We Can Break Free* (Baton Rouge: Third Millennium Press).

—— (2012) "A Public Bank for Scotland Could Ensure Economic Sovereignty." http://truth-out.org/news/item/13175-a-public -bank-for-scotland-could-ensure-economic-sovereignty

—— (2013) *The Public Bank Solution: From Austerity to Prosperity* (Baton Rouge: Third Millennium Press).

Brown, Mark (2014) *Penal Power and Colonial Rule* (London: Routledge).

Brown, Richard D. (1983) "Shays's Rebellion and Its Aftermath: A View from Springfield, Massachusetts, 1787," *The William and Mary Quarterly*, Vol. 40, No. 4: 598–615.

Broz, Laurence J. and Richard S. Grossman (2004) "Paying for Privilege: The Political Economy of Bank of England Charters, 1694-1844," *Explorations in Economic History*, Vol. 41: 48–72.

Bureau of Economic Analysis (2013) "Interest Paid and Received by Sector and Legal Form of Organization." http://www.bea.gov/histdata/ releases%5CGDP_and_PI%5C2013%5CQ2%5CThird_September-26 -2013%5CTP%5CTPsection7All_xls.xls

Burg, David F. (2004) *A World History of Tax Rebellions: An Encyclopedia of Tax Rebels, Revolts and Riots from Antiquity to the Present* (London: Routledge).

Burridge, Kenelm (1969) *New Heaven, New Earth: A Study of Millenarian Activities* (New York: Basil Blackwell).

Burton, Dawn (2008) *Credit and Consumer Society* (London: Routledge).

Büscher, Bram, Sian Sullivan, Katja Neves, Jim Igoe and Dan Brockington (2012) "Towards a Synthesized Critique of Neoliberal Biodiversity Conservation," *Capitalism Nature Socialism*, Vol. 23, No. 2: 4–30

Bush, Barbara and Josephine Maltby (2004) "Taxation in West Africa: Transforming the Colonial Subject into the 'Governable Person'," *Critical Perspectives on Accounting*, Vol. 15: 5–34.

Caffentzis, George (2013) "Reflections on the History of Debt Resistance: The Case of El Barzon," *Strike Debt*, November 19. http://strikedebt.org/elbarzon/

Cahill, Damien (2013) "Ideas-Centred Explanations of the Rise of Neoliberalism: A Critique," *Australian Journal of Political Science*, Vol. 48, No. 1: 71–84.

——— (2014) *The End of Laissez-faire: On the Durability of Embedded Neoliberalism* (Cheltenham: Edward Elgar).

Carruthers, Bruce G. (1996) *City of Capital: Politics and Markets in the English Financial Revolution* (Princeton: Princeton University Press).

Carruthers, Bruce G. and Sarah Babb (1996) "The Color of Money and the Nature of Value: Greenbacks and Gold in Postbellum America," *Journal of Sociology*, Vol. 101, No. 6: 1556–1591.

Center for Disease Control (2013) "Overweight and Obesity." http://www.cdc.gov/obesity/data/prevalence-maps.html

Center for Human Rights and Global Justice (2011) *Every Thirty Minutes: Farmer Suicides, Human Rights, and the Agrarian Crisis in India* (New York: NYU School of Law).

Chancellor, Edward (1999) *Devil Take the Hindmost: A History of Financial Speculation* (New York: Plume).

Chen, D. (2014) "Three Reasons the BRICS' New Development Bank Matters," *The Diplomat*. http://thediplomat.com/2014/07/3-reasons-the-brics-new-development-bank-matters/

Cheru, Fantu (2001) "Overcoming Apartheid's Legacy: The Ascendancy of Neoliberalism in South Africa's Anti-poverty Strategy," *Third World Quarterly*, Vol. 22, No. 4: 505–527.

Chibnik, Michael (2011) *Anthropology, Economics and Choice* (Austin: University of Texas Press).

Chorafas, Dimitris N. (2011) *Sovereign Debt Crisis: The New Normal and the Newly Poor* (Basingstoke: Palgrave MacMillan).

Chossudovsky, Michel (2002) *The Globalization of Poverty* (London: Zed).

Chua, Swee (1999) "Economic Growth, Liberalization, and the Environment: A Review of the Economic Evidence," *Annual. Review of Energy and the Environment*, Vol. 24: 391–430.

Clark, William R. (2005) *Petrodollar Warfare: Oil, Iraq, and the Future of the Dollar* (Gabriola Island: New Society Publishers).

Clay, C. G. A. (1984) *Economic Expansion and Social Change, 1500-1700: Volume 1, People, Land and Towns* (Cambridge: Cambridge University Press).

Clayton, James L. (1976) "The Fiscal Limits of the Warfare-Welfare State: Defense and Welfare Spending in the United States since 1900," *The Western Political Quarterly*, Vol. 29, No. 3: 364–383.

Cohen, Jay (1982) "The History of Imprisonment for Debt and Its Relation to the Development of Discharge in Bankruptcy," *The Journal of Legal History*, Vol. 3, No. 2: 153–171.

Corkery, Michael and Jessica Silver-Greenberg (2014) "Miss a Payment? Good Luck Moving That Car," *New York Times*, September 24. http://dealbook. nytimes.com/2014/09/24/miss-a-payment-good-luck-moving-that-car/
——— (2015) "Investment Riches Built on Subprime Auto Loans to Poor," *New York Times*, January 26. http://dealbook.nytimes.com/2015/01/26/ investment-riches-built-on-auto-loans-to-poor/?hp&action=click&pgt ype=Homepage&module=first-column-region&region=top-news&WT. nav=top-news&_r=0

Costanza, Robert, et al. (2009) *Beyond GDP: The Need for New Measures of Progress*. The Pardee Papers # 4. Boston University. http://www.oecd.org/ site/progresskorea/globalproject/42613423.pdf

Cowen, David Jack (2000) *The Origins and Economic Impact of the First Bank of the United States, 1791–1797* (New York: Garland Publishing).

Credit Suisse (2013) *Global Wealth Report 2013*. October (Switzerland: CREDIT SUISSE AG Research Institute) https://publications.credit-suisse. com/tasks/render/file/?fileID=BCDB1364-A105-0560-1332EC9100FF5C83.

Creutz, Helmut (2010) *The Money Syndrome* (Peterborough: Upfront Publishing).

Curtis, Thomas D. (2014) "Editor's Introduction: Updating the Curtis Thesis' and Riches, Real Estate, and Resistance: How Land Speculation, Debt, and Trade Monopolies Led to the American Revolution," *American Journal of Economics and Sociology*, Vol. 73: 445–626.

Daly, Herman (1997) *Beyond Growth: The Economics of Sustainable Development* (New York: Beacon Press).
——— (2005) "Economics in a Crowded World," *Scientific American*, Vol. 293: 100–107.
——— (2008) "A Steady-State Economy." Sustainable Development Commission, UK. http://steadystaterevolution.org/files/pdf/Daly_UK _Paper.pdf

Davies, Glyn (2002) *A History of Money: From Ancient Times to the Present Day* (Cardiff: University of Wales Press).

Davis, Mike (2007) *Planet of Slums* (London: Verso).

Decker, Oliver (2014) *Commodified Bodies: Organ Transplantation and the Organ Trade* (London: Routledge).

Denby, Charles (1916) "The National Debt of China-Its Origin and Its Security," *Annals of the American Academy of Political and Social Science*, Vol. 68: 55–70.

Deshpande, R. S. and Saroj Arora (eds) (2010) *Agrarian Crisis and Farmer Suicides* (New Delhi: SAGE Publications).

de Vries, Jan and Ad van der Woude (1997) *The First Modern Economy: Success, Failure, and Perseverance of the Dutch Economy, 1500–1815* (Cambridge: Cambridge University Press).

Dickson, P. G. M. (1967) *The Financial Revolution in England: A Study in the Development of Public Credit, 1688–1756* (New York: St. Martin's Press).

Dienst, Richard (2011) *The Bonds of Debt: Borrowing against the Common Good* (London: Verso).

Di Muzio, Tim (2007) "The Art of Colonization: The Capitalization of the State and the Ongoing Nature of Primitive Accumulation," *New Political Economy*, Vol. 12, No. 4: 517–539.

—— (2012) "Capitalizing a Future Unsustainable: Finance, Energy and the Fate of Market Civilization," *Review of International Political Economy*, Vol. 19, No. I. 3: 363–388.

—— (ed.) (2014) *The Capitalist Mode of Power: Critical Engagements with the Power Theory of Value* (London: Routledge).

—— (2015) *The 1% and the Rest of Us: A Political Economy of Dominant Ownership* (London: Zed Press).

Dobbs, Richard, et al. (2015) *Debt and (not much) Deleveraging* (McKinsey and Company). http://www.mckinsey.com/insights/economic_studies/debt _and_not_much_deleveraging (accessed April 17, 2015).

Dorling, Danny (2014) *Inequality and the 1%* (London: Verso).

Douthwaite, Richard (2010) "Money and Energy," in Heinberg, Richard. and Daniel Lerch (eds.) *The Post-Carbon Reader: Managing the 21st Century Sustainability Crises* (Berkeley: University of California Press): 279–283.

Dyer, Christopher (1997) "The *Howard Linecar Lecture 1997*. Peasants and Coins: The Uses of Money in the Middle Ages," *British Numismatic Journal*, Vol. 67: 30–47.

Edling, Max M. and Mark D. Kaplanoff (2004) "Alexander Hamilton's Fiscal Reform: Transforming the Structure of Taxation in the Early Republic," *William and Mary Quarterly*, Vol. 61, No. 4: 713–744.

El Diwany, Tarek (1997) *The Problem with Interest* (London: TA-HA Publishers).

El-Gamal, Mahmoud A. and Amy Myers Jaffe (2010) *Oil, Dollars, Debt and Crises: The Global Curse of Black Gold* (Cambridge: Cambridge University Press).

Engdahl, William (2004) *A Century of War: Anglo-American Oil Politics and the New World Order* (London: Pluto Press).

Evans, Emory G. (1962) "Planter Indebtedness and the Coming of the Revolution in Virginia," *The William and Mary Quarterly*, Vol. 19, No. 4: 511–533.

Federal Trade Commission (2013) "The Structure and Practices of the Debt Buying Industry." http://www.ftc.gov/sites/default/files/documents/reports/structure-and-practices-debt-buying-industry/debtbuyingreport.pdf (accessed April 17, 2015).

Federici, Silvia (2003) *Caliban and the Witch: Women, the Body and Primitive Accumulation* (New York and London: Autonomedia; Pluto).

Felsenheimer, Jochen and Philip Gisdakis (2008) *Credit Crisis: From Tainted Loans to a Global Economic Meltdown* (Weinheim: Wiley-VCH).

Ferguson, E. James (1954) "Speculation in the Revolutionary Debt: The Ownership of Public Securities in Maryland, 1790," *The Journal of Economic History*, Vol. 14: 35–45.

—— (1979) *The American Revolution: A General History, 1763–1790* (Homewood: The Dorsey Press).

Ferguson, Niall (1998) *The House of Rothschild: Money's Prophets, 1798–1848* (London: Penguin Books).

—— (2001) *The Cash Nexus: Money and Power in the Modern World, 1700–2000* (New York: Basic Books).

—— (2008) *The Ascent of Money* (New York: Penguin Press).

Financial Times (2009) 'A Survival Plan for Global Capitalism,' March 8.

Fioramonti, Lorenzo (2013) *Gross Domestic Problem: The Politics behind the World's Most Powerful Number* (London: Zed Books).

Forstater, Matthew (2005) "Taxation and Primitive Accumulation: The Case of Colonial Africa," *Research in Political Economy*, Vol. 22: 51–65.

Foucault, Michel (2004) *The Birth of Biopolitics: Lectures at the College de France* (New York: Picador).

Fraser, Steve (2005) *Every Man a Speculator: A History of Wall Street in American Life* (New York: Harper Perennial).

Freeland, Chrystia (2012) *Plutocrats: The Rise of the New Global Super-Rich and the Fall of Everyone Else* (New York: Penguin).

Fresia, Jerry (1988) *Toward an American Revolution* (Boston: South End Press).

Friedenberg, Daniel M. (1992) *Life, Liberty and the Pursuit of Land: The Plunder of Early America* (Buffalo: Prometheus Books).

Friedman, Benjamin M. (2005) *The Moral Consequences of Economic Growth* (New York: Vintage).

Galbraith, John Kenneth (2010) *John Kenneth Galbraith: The Affluent Society and Other Writings 1952–1967* (Des Moines, IA: The Library of America).

Gardner, Brian (2013) *Global Food Futures: Feeding the World in 2050* (London: Bloomsbury Academic).

Garson, Barbara (2001) *Money Makes the World Go Around: One Investor Tracks Her Cash through the Global Economy* (New York: Penguin).

Geisst, Charles R. (2013) *Beggar Thy Neighbor: A History of Usury and Debt* (Philadelphia: University of Pennsylvania Press).

Gelles, David (2014) "An Employee Dies, and the Company Collects the Insurance," *New York Times*, June 22. http://dealbook.nytimes.com/2014/06/22/an-employee-dies-and-the-company-collects-the-insurance/?_r=0

Gellner, Ernest (1983) *Nations and Nationalism* (Ithaca: Cornell University Press).

Gelpi, Rosa-Maria and François Julien-Labruyère (2000) *The History of Consumer Credit: Doctrines and Practices* (New York: St. Martin's Press).

Gendell, Murry (2006) "Full Time Work among the Elderly Increases," *Population Reference Bureau*. http://www.prb.org/Publications/Articles/2006/FullTimeWorkAmongElderlyIncreases.aspx (accessed April 17, 2015).

George, Susan (1988) *A Fate Worse than Debt* (London: Penguin).

——— (1992) *The Debt Boomerang: How Third World Debt Harms Us All* (London: Pluto Press).

Gerber, Julien-François (2014) "The role of rural indebtedness in the evolution of capitalism." *Journal of Peasant Studies* 41.5 (2014): 729–747.

Gilbert, Emily and Eric Helleiner (eds) (1999) *Nation-States and Money: The Past, Present and Future of National Currencies* (London: Routledge).

Gilens, Martin and Benjamin I. Page (2014) "Testing Theories of American Politics: Elites, Interest Groups, and Average Citizens," *Perspective on Politics*, Vol. 12: 564–581.

Gill, Stephen (1995) "Globalization, Market Civilisation & Disciplinary Neoliberalism," *Millennium: Journal of International Studies*, Vol. 24, No. 3: 399–423.

——— (ed.) (2012) *Global Crises and the Crisis of Global Leadership* (Cambridge: Cambridge University Press).

——— (ed.) (2013) *Global Crises and the Crisis of Global Leadership* (Cambridge: Cambridge University Press).

Gish, Steven (2004) *Desmond Tutu: A Biography* (Portland: Greenwood).

Glaeser, Edward L. (2011) "Goodbye, Golden Years," *New York Times*, November 20. http://www.nytimes.com/2011/11/20/opinion/sunday/retirement-goodbye-golden-years.html?pagewanted=all&_r=0

Gleick, James (2000) *Faster: The Acceleration of Just about Everything* (New York: Vintage).

Glover, Paul (1995) *Hometown Money: How to Enrich Your Community with Local Currency* (Ithaca: Ithaca Money).

Goldstone, Jack A. (2002) "Efflorescences and Economic Growth in World History: Rethinking the 'Rise of the West' and the Industrial Revolution," *Journal of World History*, Vol. 13, No. 2: 323–389.

Gowan, Peter (1999) *The Global Gamble: Washington's Bid for Global Dominance* (London: Verso).

Graeber, David (2009) *Direct Action: An Ethnography* (Oakland: AK Press).

—— (2011) *Debt: The First 5,000 Years* (New York: Melville House).

—— (2013) "After the Jubilee." http://www.e-flux.com/wp-content/uploads/2013/05/2.-Graeber_afterJubilee.pdf (accessed April 17, 2015).

Greene, Jack P. and Richard M. Jellison (1961) "The Currency Act of 1764 in Imperial-Colonial Relations, 1764-1776," *The William and Mary Quarterly*, Vol. 18, No. 4: 485–518.

Greer, Scott (2014) "Structural Adjustment Comes to Europe: Lessons for the Eurozone from the Conditionality Debates," *Global Social Policy*, Vol. 14, No. 1: 51–71.

Griffith-Jones, Stephany (1989) *Third World Debt: Managing the Consequences* (London: IFR Publishing).

Gunder, Frank, A. (1976) *On Capitalist Underdevelopment* (Oxford: University of Oxford Press).

Hager, Sandy Brian (2013) "What Happened to the Bondholding Class? Public Debt, Power and the Top One Per Cent," *New Political Economy*, Vol. 19, No. 2: 155–182.

Hall, Charles A. S. and Kent A. Klitgaard (2012) *Energy and the Wealth of Nations: Understanding the Biophysical Economy* (New York: Springer).

Hall, Mike (1988) "The International Debt Crisis: Recent Developments," *Capital and Class*, Vol. 12, No. 2: 7–18.

Hallsmith, Gwendolyn and Bernard Lietaer (2011) *Creating Wealth: Growing Local Economies with Local Currencies* (Gabriola Island: New Society Publishers).

Halpern, Jake (2014) *Bad Paper: Chasing Debt from Wall Street to the Underworld* (New York: Farrar Straus and Giroux). See also "Paper Boys; Inside the Dark Labyrinthine, and Extremely Lucrative World of Consumer Debt Collection," *New York Times Magazine*. August 15. http://www.nytimes.com/interactive/2014/08/15/magazine/bad-paper-debt-collector.html

Hamilton, Clive (2004) *Growth Fetish* (London: Pluto Press).

Hamilton, Earl J. (1947) "Origin and Growth of the National Debt in Western Europe," *The American Economic Review*, Vol. 37, No. 2: 118–130.

Hamilton, J. D. (2009) "Causes and Consequences of the Oil Shock of 2007-8," *Brookings Papers on Economic Activity*, Spring: 215–261 http://www.brookings.edu/~/media/Files/Programs/ES/BPEA/2009_spring_bpea_papers/2009_spring_bpea_hamilton.pdf (8/31/2014)

Hammond, John Craig (2003) "'We Are to Be Reduced to the Level of Slaves': Planters, Taxes, Aristocrats, and Massachusetts Antifederalists, 1787–1788," *Historical Journal of Massachusetts*, Vol. 31, No. 2: 172–198.

Harbaugh, William, Arik Levinson and David Molloy Wilson (2002) "Reexamining the Empirical Evidence for an Environmental Kuznets Curve," *The Review of Economics and Statistics*, Vol. 84: 541–551.

Häring, Norbert (2013) "The Veil of Deception over Money: How Central Bankers and Textbooks Distort the Nature of Banking and Central Banking," *Real-World Economics Review*, No. 64: 1–17.

Hartwick Elaine, Richard Peet (2003) "Neoliberalism and Nature: The Case of the WTO," *Annals of the American Academy of Political and Social Science*, Vol. 590: 188–211.

Harvey, David (2005) *A Brief History of Neoliberalism* (London: Oxford University Press).

—— (2010) *The Enigma of Capital: The Crises of Capitalism* (Oxford: Oxford University Press).

—— (2014) *Seventeen Contradictions and the End of Capitalism* (Oxford: Oxford University Press).

Hayward, Joel (1995) "Hitler's Quest for Oil: The Impact of Economic Considerations on Military Strategy, 1941–42," *Journal of Strategic Studies*, Vol. 18, No. 4: 94–135.

Heinberg, Richard (2003) *The Party's Over: Oil, War and the Fate of Industrial Societies* (Gabriola Island: New Society Publishers).

—— (2009) *Searching for a Miracle: "Net Energy" Limits and the Fate of Industrial Society* (International Forum on Globalization and the Post

Carbon Institute): 1–83. http://www.ifg.org/pdf/Searching%20for%20a%20 Miracle_web10nov09.pdf

——— (2011) *The End of Growth: Adapting to Our New Economic Reality* (Gabriola Island: New Society Publishers).

Heinberg, Richard and Daniel Lerch (eds) (2010) *The Post-Carbon Reader: Managing the 21st Century Sustainability Crises* (Berkeley: University of California Press).

Helleiner, Eric (2002a) "The Monetary Dimensions of Colonialism: Why Did Imperial Powers Create Currency Blocks?," *Geopolitics*, Vol. 7, No. 1: 5–30.

——— (2002b) *The Making of Modern Money: Territorial Currencies in Historical Perspective* (Ithaca, NY: Cornell University Press).

——— (2005) "The Strange Story of Bush and the Argentine Debt Crisis," *Third World Quarterly*, Vol. 26, No. 6: 951–969.

Henry, James S. (2003) *The Blood Bankers* (New York: Four Walls Eight Windows).

Henwood, Doug (1997) *Wall Street: How It Works and for Whom* (London: Verso).

Hermann, Robin (2011) "Empire Builders and Mushroom Gentlemen: The Meaning of Money in Colonial Nigeria," *International Journal of African Historical Studies*, Vol. 44, No. 3: 393–413.

Hertz, Noreena (2004) *The Debt Threat: How Debt Is Destroying the Developing World* (New York: Harper Business).

Hickel, Jason (2014) "Aid in Reverse: How Poor Countries Develop Rich Countries," *New Left Project*. http://www.newleftproject.org/index.php/ site/article_comments/aid_in_reverse_how_poor_countries_develop _rich_countries (accessed April 17, 2015).

Ho, Karen (2009) *Liquidated: An Ethnography of Wall Street* (Durham: Duke University Press).

Hobson, John (2005) *Imperialism: A Study* (New York: Cosimo).

Holland, Peter A. (2014) "Junk Justice: A Statistical Analysis of 4,400 Lawsuits Filed by Debt Buyers," *U of Maryland Legal Studies Research Paper No. 2014–13. Loyola Consumer Law Review*, Vol. 26: 179.

Holton, Woody (1999) *Forced Founders: Indians, Debtors, Slaves and the Making of the American Revolution in Virginia* (Chapel Hill: University of North Carolina Press).

——— (2004) " 'From the Labours of Other': The War Bonds Controversy and the Origins of the Constitution in New England," *The William and Mary Quarterly*, Vol. 61, No. I. 2: 271–316.

—— (2005a) "An 'Excess of Democracy'—or a Shortage?," *Journal of the Early Republic*, Vol. 25, No. 3: 339–382.

—— (2005b) "Divide et Impera: Federalist 10 in a Wider Sphere," *The William and Mary Quarterly*, Vol. 62, No. I. 2: 175–212.

Horsefield, Keith J. (1960) *British Monetary Experiments, 1650–1710* (Cambridge, MA: Harvard University Press).

Howard, James L. (2007) *U.S. Timber Production, Trade, Consumption and Price Statistics 1965 to 2005*. Research Paper FPL-RP-637. United States Department of Agriculture. http://postcom.org/eco/sls.docs/USFS-US%20 Timber%20Prod,%20Trade,%20Consumption.pdf

Hudson, Michael ([1972] 2003) *Super-Imperialism: The Origin and Fundamentals of U.S. World Dominance* (London: Pluto Press).

Hunter, Stuart (2014) "Debt Collectors Have Figured Out a Way to Seize Your Wages and Savings," *Huntington Post*, June 2. http://www.huffingtonpost .com/2014/06/02/debt-collectors-wages-savings_n_5364062.html

Igoe, Jim and Dan Brockington (2007) "Neoliberal Conservation: A Brief Introduction," *Conservation and Society*, Vol. 5: 432–449.

ILO (2013) *Global Employment Trends for Youth 2013* (International Labor Organization). http://www.ilo.org/global/research/global-reports/global -employment-trends/youth/2013/lang--en/index.htm

Indiviglio, Daniel (2011) "Chart of the Day: Student Loans Have Grown 511% since 1999," *The Atlantic*, August 18. http://www.theatlantic.com/ business/archive/2011/08/chart-of-the-day-student-loans-have-grown -511-since-1999/243821/

Ingham, Geoffrey (1999) "Capitalism, Money and Banking: A Critique of Recent Historical Sociology," *British Journal of Sociology*, Vol. 50, No. 1: 76–98.

—— (2004) *The Nature of Money* (Cambridge: Polity Press).

IPCC (2014) *Climate Change 2014: Impacts, Adaptation, and Vulnerability. Summary for Policymakers*. https://ipcc-wg2.gov/AR5/images/uploads/ IPCC_WG2AR5_SPM_Approved.pdf (accessed April 17, 2015).

Jackson, Andrew and Ben Dyson (2013) *Modernizing Money: Why Our Monetary System Is Broken and How It Can be Fixed* (London: Positive Money).

Jackson, Tim (2009) *Prosperity without Growth: Economics for a Finite Planet* (London: Earthscan).

Jeffries, Sheila (2009) *The Industrial Vagina: The Political Economy of the Global Sex Trade* (London: Routledge).

Johnson, Simon and James Kwak (2012) *White House Burning: The Founding Fathers, Our National Debt, and Why It Matter to You* (New York: Pantheon Books).

Johnston, David Cay (ed.) (2014) *Divided: The Perils of Our Growing Inequality* (New York: The New Press).

Jones, Charles (2002) *Introduction to Economic Growth* (New York: W.W. Norton & Company).

Jones, Van (2012) *Rebuilding the Dream* (New York: Nation Books).

Kaiser, Robert G. (2010) *So Damn Much Money: The Triumph of Lobbying and the Corrosion of American Government* (New York: Vintage).

Kempf, Hervé (2008) *How the Rich Are Destroying the Earth*. Translated by Leslie Thatcher (Foxhole: Green Books).

Kennedy, Margrit (2012) *Occupy Money: Creating an Economy Where Everybody Wins* (Philadelphia: New Society Publishers).

—— (1995) *Interest and Inflation-Free Money*. http://userpage.fu -berlin.de/~roehrigw/kennedy/english/Interest-and-inflation-free-money .pdf (accessed April 17, 2015).

Kennedy, Margrit and Declan Kennedy (1995) *Interest and Inflation Free Money: Creating an Exchange Medium That Works for Everyone and Protects the Earth* (Philadelphia: New Society Publishers).

Keucheyan, Razmig (2014) "The French Are Right: Tear up the Public Debt – Most of It Is Illegitimate Anyway," *The Guardian*, UK, June 10.

Killingray, David (1986) "The Maintenance of Law and Order in British Colonial Africa," *African Affairs*, Vol. 85, No. 340: 411–437.

Kim, Jongchul (2012) *How Politics Shaped Modern Banking in Early Modern England Rethinking the Nature of Representative Democracy, Public Debt, and Modern Banking*. MPIfG Discussion Paper 12/11. http://www.mpifg .de/pu/mpifg_dp/dp12-11.pdf (accessed April 17, 2015).

Kindleberger, Charles (1996) *World Economic Primacy, 1500–1900* (Oxford: Oxford University Press).

Kindleberger, Charles and Robert Z. Aliber (2005) *Manias, Panics and Crashes: A History of Financial Crises* (Basingstoke: Palgrave MacMillan).

King, Frank H. H. (2006) "The Boxer Indemnity—'Nothing but Bad'," *Modern Asian Studies*, Vol. 40: 663–689.

Klein, Naomi (2010) "Haiti: A Creditor, Not a Debtor." http://www.naomiklein .org/articles/2010/02/haiti-creditor-not-debtor (4/1/2012).

—— (2014) *This Changes Everything: Capitalism vs. The Climate* (New York: Simon & Schuster).

Konings, Martijn (2011) *The Development of American Finance* (Cambridge: Cambridge University Press).

Korten, David C. (1995) *When Corporations Rule the World* (Hartford, CT: Kumarian Press).

Kouvelakis, Stathis (2011) "The Greek Cauldron," *New Left Review*, Vol. 72: 17–32.

Kroll, Gary and Richard H. Robbins (2009) *Worlds in Motion: The Globalization and Environment Reader* (Washington: AltaMira Press).

Kubursi, A. A. and S. Mansur (1994) "The Political Economy of Middle Eastern Oil," in Stubbs, Richard and Geoffrey R.D. Underhill (eds) *Political Economy and the Changing Global Order* (Toronto: Oxford University Press): 313–327.

Kuhner, Timothy K. (2014) *Capitalism V. Democracy: Money in Politics and the Free Market Constitution* (Stanford, CA: Stanford Law Books).

Kumar, Ravinder (2011) "The Deccan Riots of 1875," *The Journal of Asian Studies*, Vol. 24, No. I. 4: 613–635.

Kuznets, Simon and Elizabeth Jenks (1953) *Shares of Upper Income Groups in Income and Savings* (New York: National Bureau of Economic Research).

Kwarteng, Kwasi (2014) *War and Gold: A 500 Year History of Empires, Adventures and Debt* (London: Bloomsbury).

Lane, Philip R. (2012) "The European Sovereign Debt Crisis," *The Journal of Economic Perspectives*, Vol. 26, No. 3: 49–67.

Lazzarato, Maurizio (2012) *The Making of the Indebted Man* (Cambridge, MA: MIT Press).

LeBaron, Genevieve and Adrienne Roberts (2012) "Confining Social Insecurity: Neoliberalism and the Rise of the 21st Century Debtors' Prison," *Politics and Gender*, Vol. 8, No. 1: 25–49.

Leonard, Annie (2011) *The Story of Stuff* (New York: Free Press).

Levien, Michael (2011) "Special Economic Zones and Accumulation by Dispossession in India," *Journal of Agrarian Change*, Vol. 11, No. 4: 454–483.

—— (2012) "The Land Question: Special Economic Zones and the Political Economy of Dispossession in India," *Journal of Peasant Studies*, Vol. 39, No. 3–4: 933–969.

—— (2013) "The Politics of Dispossession: Theorizing India's 'Land Wars,'" *Politics & Society*, Vol. 41, No. 3: 351–394.

Lewis, W. Arthur (1955) *The Theory of Economic Growth* (London: George Allen & Unwin).

Lietaer, Bernard (2006) "A Proposal for a Brazilian Education Complementary Currency," *International Journal of Community Currency Research*, Vol. 10: 18–23.

Lietaer, Bernard A. and Jacqui Dunne (2013) *Rethinking Money: How New Currencies Turn Scarcity into Prosperity* (San Francisco: Berrett-Koehler Publishers, Inc.).

Lin, Shuanglin (2003) "China's Government Debt: How Serious?," *China: An International Journal*, Vol. 1, No. 1: 73–98.

Loubert, Aart (2012) "Sovereign Debt Threatens the Union: The Genesis of a Federation," *European Constitutional Law Review*, Vol. 8, No. 3: 442–455.

MacEwan, Arthur (1990) *Debt and Disorder* (New York: Monthly Review Press).

Maddison, Angus (2001) *The World Economy: A Millennial Perspective* (Paris: Development Centre of the Organization for Economic Co-operation and Development).

Madrick, Jeff (2002) *Why Economies Grow: The Forces That Shape Prosperity and How We Can Get the Working Again* (New York: Basic Books).

Mahmud, Tayyab (2011) "Is It Greek or Deja Vu All over Again: Neoliberalism and Winners and Losers of International Debt Crises," *Loyola University of Chicago Law Journal*, Vol. 42, No. 4: 629–712.

—— (2012) "Debt and Discipline," *American Quarterly*, Vol. 64, No. 3: 469–494.

Mankiw, Gregory N. (2013) "Defending the One Percent," *The Journal of Economic Perspectives*, Vol. 27: 21–34 (see also http://scholar.harvard.edu/files/mankiw/files/defending_the_one_percent.pdf)

Mann, Bruce H. (2003) *Republic of Debtors: Bankruptcy in the Age of American Independence* (Cambridge, MA: Harvard University Press).

Manning, Robert D. (2001) *Credit Card Nation* (New York: Basic Books).

Manolopoulos, Jason (2011) *Greece's Odious Debt* (London: Anthem Press).

Marcuse, Herber (1972) *Counterrevolution and Revolt* (Boston: Beacon Press).

Marks, Shula (1970) *Reluctant Rebellion* (Oxford: Clarendon Press).

Martenson, Chris (2011) *The Crash Course: The Unsustainable Future of Our Economy, Energy and Environment* (Hoboken: John Wiley & Sons).

Marx, Karl (1887) *Capital: A Critique of Political Economy Volume 1*. Translated by Samuel Moore and Edward Aveling (Moscow: Progress Publishers).

—— (1981) *Capital Volume 3: A Critique of Political Economy*. Translated by David Fernbach (New York: Penguin Putnam).

McAfee, K. (1999) "Selling Nature to Save It? Biodiversity and Green Developmentalism," *Society and Space*, Vol. 17, No. 2: 203–219.

McCartney, Matthew (2005) "Neoliberalism in South Asia: The Case of a Narrowing Discourse," in Saad-Filho, Alfredo and Deborah Johnston (eds) *Neoliberalism: A Critical Reader* (London: Pluto Press): 2137–2244.

McKibben, Bill (2007) *Deep Economy: The Wealth of Communities and the Durable Future* (New York: Times Books).

McKinsey Global Institute (2013) *Financial Globalization: Retreat or Reset*. March. http://www.mckinsey.com/insights/global_capital_markets/financial_globalization

—— (2015) *Debt and (not much) Deleveraging* (McKinsey Global Institute). http://www.mckinsey.com/insights/economic_studies/debt_and_not_much_deleveraging (accessed April 17, 2015).

McNeill, J. R. (2000) *Something New under the Sun: An Environmental History of the Twentieth-Century World* (New York: W. W. Norton & Company).

Mellor, Mary (2010) *The Future of Money: From Financial Crisis to Public Resource* (London: Pluto Press).

Metcalf, Thomas R. (1962) "The British and the Moneylender in Nineteenth-Century India," *The Journal of Modern History*, Vol. 34, No. 4: 390–397.

Michael, Kremer and Seema Jayachandran (2002) "Odious Debt," *Finance and Development*, Vol. 39, No. 2. http://www.imf.org/external/pubs/ft/fandd/2002/06/kremer.htm

Micklethwait, John and Adrian Wooldrige (2003) *The Company: A Short History of a Revolutionary Idea* (New York: Modern Library).

Miller, Daniel, Michael Rowlands, and Christopher Tilley (eds) (1995) *Domination and Resistance* (London: Routledge).

Mishan, E. J. (1967) *The Costs of Economic Growth* (Harmondsworth: Staples Press).

Mohanty, B. B. (2005) "'We Are Like the Living Dead': Farmer Suicides in Maharashtra, Western India," *The Journal of Peasant Studies*, Vol. 32, No. 2: 243–276.

Moniruzzaman, Monir (2012) "'Living Cadavers' in Bangladesh: Bioviolence in the Human Organ Bazaar," *Medical Anthropology Quarterly*, Vol. 26, No. I. 1: 69–91.

Montgomerie, Johnna (2006) "The Financialization of the American Credit Card Industry," *Competition and Change*, Vol. 10, No. 3: 301–319.

—— (2009) "The Pursuit of (Past) Happiness," *New Political Economy*, Vol. 14, No. 1: 1–24.

—— (2013) "America's Debt Safety Net," *Public Administration*, Vol. 91, No. 4: 871–888.

Morris, Richard B. (1962) "Class Struggle and the American Revolution," *The William and Mary Quarterly*, Vol. 19, No. 1: 3–29.

Moss, Michael (2013) *Salt, Sugar, Fat: How the Food Giants Hooked Us* (New York: Random House).

Muldrew, Craig (1998) *The Economy of Obligation: The Culture of Credit and Social Relations in Early Modern England* (London: Palgrave).

Mwangi, Wambui (2001) "Of Coins and Conquest: The East African Currency Board, the Rupee Crisis, and the Problem of Colonialism in the East African Protectorate," *Comparative Studies in Society and History*, Vol. 43: 763–787.

—— (2004) "Of Coins and Conquest: The East African Currency Board, the Rupee Crisis, and the Problem of Colonialism in the East African Protectorate," *Society for Comparative Study of Society and History*, Vol. 43, No. I. 4: 763–787.

Naylor, R. T. (1994) *Hot Money and the Politics of Debt* (Montreal: Black Rose Books).

Ndikumana, Léonce and James K. Boyce (2011) *Africa's Odious Debts: How Foreign Loans and Capital Flight Bled a Continent* (London: Zed Books).

Nedelsky, Jennifer (1990) *Private Property and the Limits of American Constitutionalism: The Madisonian Framework and Its Legacy* (Chicago: The University of Chicago Press).

Nef, John U. (November, 1977) "An Early Energy Crisis and Its Consequences," *Scientific American*, Vol. 237: 140–150.

Nehru, Jawaharlal (1946) *The Discovery of India* (New York: John Day Company).

Niemi, Johanna, Iain Ramsay and William Whitford (eds) (2009) *Consumer Credit, Debt and Bankruptcy: Comparative and International Perspectives* (Portland, OR: Hart Publishing).

Nitzan, Jonathan (2001) "Regimes of Differential Accumulation: Mergers, Stagflation and the Logic of Globalization," *Review of International Political Economy*, Vol. 8, No. 2: 226–274.

Nitzan, Jonathan and Shimshon Bichler (2009) *Capital as Power: A Study of Order and Creorder* (London: Routledge).

Nkrumah, Kwame (1965) *Neo-Colonialism, The Last Stage of Imperialism* (London: Thomas Nelson & Sons).

Noah, Timothy (2012) *The Great Divergence: America's Growing Inequality Crisis and What We Can Do About It* (London: Bloomsbury Press).

North, Douglass and Barry Weingast (1989) "Constitutions and Commitment: The Evolution of Institutions Governing Public Choice in Seventeenth-Century England," *Journal of Economic History*, Vol. 49: 803–832.

North, Peter (2007) *Money and Liberation: The Micropolitics of Alternative Currency Movements* (Minneapolis: University of Minnesota Press).

—— (2014) "Ten Square Miles Surrounded by Reality? Materialising Alternative Economies Using Local Currencies," *Antipode*, Vol. 46, No. 1: 246–265.

Nyerere, Julius K. (1985) "Africa and the Debt Crisis," *African Affairs*, Vol. 84, No. 337: 489–497.

O'Brien, Patrick K. (1988) "The Political Economy of British Taxation, 1660–1815," *The Economic History Review*, Vol. 41, No. 1: 1–32.

O'Connor, James O. (1998) *Natural Causes: Essays in Ecological Marxism* (New York: Guilford Press).

OECD (2014) *Pension Markets in Focus*. http://www.oecd.org/daf/fin/private-pensions/Pension-Markets-in-Focus-2014.pdf (accessed April 17, 2015).

Ofonagoro, Walter I. (1979) "From Traditional to British Currency in Southern Nigeria: Analysis of a Currency Revolution," *The Journal of Economic History*, Vol. 39, No. 3: 623–654.

Oliver, Roland and G. N. Sanderson (1985) *Cambridge History of Africa*, Volume 6: 1870–1905 (Cambridge: Cambridge University Press).

Olmos Gaona, Alejandro (2001) "The Illegal Foreign Debt: The Value and Likelihood of a Legal Ruling," Paper prepared for the International Jubilee 2000 Conference Bamako, Mali, April 21–23.

Omond, T. S. (1870) *The National Debt: Its Origins and Political Significance* (Oxford: Oxford University Press).

Oppenheim, V. H. (1976–7) "Why Oil Prices Go Up? The Past: We Pushed Them," *Foreign Policy*, No. 25: 24–57.

Oxfam (2015) *Wealth: Having It All and Wanting More*. Oxfam Issue Briefing. http://policy-practice.oxfam.org.uk/publications/wealth-having-it-all-and-wanting-more-338125

Pakenham, Thomas (1992) *The Scramble for Africa* (London: Abacus).

Palast, Greg (2014) "The Vulture: Chewing Argentina's Living Corpse," *Greg Palast: Journalism and Film*. July 30. http://www.gregpalast.com/the-vulture-chewing-argentinas-living-corpse/

Papavasiliou, Faidra (2008) *The Political Economy of Local Currency: Alternative Money, Alternative Development and Collective Action in the Age of Globalization*. A dissertation submitted to the Faculty of the Graduate School of Emory University in partial fulfillment of the requirements for the degree of Doctor of Philosophy.

—— (2010) "Fair Money, Fair Trade: Tracing Alternative Consumption in a Local Currency Economy," in Sarah Lyon and Mark Moberg, eds. *Fair Trade and Social Justice* (New York: New York University Press): 202–228.

Patel, Raj (2009) *The Value of Nothing* (Melbourne: Black Inc. Publishing).

Payer, Cheryl (1974) *The Debt Trap: The Third World and the IMF* (Harmondsworth: Penguin Books).

Pendergrast, Mark (1999) *Uncommon Grounds: The History of Coffee and How It Transformed Our World* (New York: Basic Books).

Perelman, Michael (2000) *The Invention of Capitalism: Classical Political Economy and the Secret History of Primitive Accumulation* (Durham: Duke University Press).

Perkins, John (2004) *Confessions of an Economic Hit Man* (San Francisco: Berrett-Koehler Publishers).

Pettifor, Ann (2006) *The Coming First World Debt Crisis* (Basingstoke: Palgrave MacMillan).

—— (2014) *Just Money: How Society Can Break the Despotic Power of Finance* (London: Commonwealth).

Philippon, Thomas (2014) *Has the U.S. Finance Industry Become Less Efficient? On the Theory and Measurement of Financial Intermediation* (Stern School of Business, New York University). http://pages.stern.nyu.edu/~tphilipp/papers/Finance_Efficiency.pdf or http://www.russellsage.org/sites/all/files/Rethinking-Finance/Philippon_v3.pdf

Piketty, Thomas (2014) *Capital in the Twenty-First Century* (Cambridge, MA: Belknap Press).

Pipes, Richard (1999) *Property and Freedom* (New York: Alfred A. Knopf).

Podobnik, Bruce (2006) *Global Energy Shifts: Fostering Sustainability in a Turbulent Age* (Philadelphia: Temple University Press).

Polanyi, Karl ([1944] 1957) *The Great Transformation: The Political and Economic Origins of Our Time* (Boston: Beacon Press).

Pollan, Michael (2007) *The Omnivore's Dilemma: A Natural History of Four Meals* (New York: Penguin).

Prashad, Vijay (2007) *The Darker Nations: A People's History of the Third World* (New York: The New Press).

ProPublica: Journalism in the Public Interest (2015) *Bailout Tracker*. http://projects.propublica.org/bailout/list (accessed April 17, 2015).

Putnam, Robert (2000) *Bowling Alone: The Collapse and Revival of American Community* (New York: Simon & Schuster).

Raine, Kim D. (2012) 'Obesity Epidemics: Inevitable Outcome of Globalization or Preventable Public Health Challenge?," *International Journal of Public Health*, Vol. 57, Vol. I. 1: 35–36.

Ratcliffe, Caroline, Signe-Mary McKernan, Brett Theodos, Emma Kalish, John Chalekian, Peifang Guo and Christopher Trepel (2014) *Delinquent Debt in America. Urban Institute and Consumer Credit Research Institute*, Encore Capital Group. http://www.urban.org/UploadedPDF/413191-Delinquent -Debt-in-America.pdf (accessed April 17, 2015).

Redding, Sean (2000) "A Blood-Stained Tax: Poll Tax and the Bambatha Rebellion in South Africa," *African Studies Review*, Vol. 43, No. 2: 29–54.

Reddy, Sudeep (2013) "Number of the Week: Total World Debt Load at 313% of GDP," *Wall Street Journal*, May 11. http://blogs.wsj.com/ economics/2013/05/11/number-of-the-week-total-world-debt-load-at -313-of-gdp/

Reich, Robert B. (2012) *Beyond Outrage: Expanded Edition: What Has Gone Wrong with Our Economy and Our Democracy, and How to Fix It* (New York: Vintage).

Reinhart, Carmen M. and Keneth S. Rogoff (2009) *This Time Is Different: Eight Centuries of Financial Folly* (Princeton: Princeton University Press).

Research and Markets; Global Credit Card Industry—Emerging Markets (2010) *Asia Business Newsweekly*, p. 336.

Rifkin, Mark (2008) "Debt and the Transnationalization of Hawai'i," *American Quarterly*, Vol. 60, No. 1: 43–66.

Rist, Gilbert (2008) *The History of Development: From Western Origins to Global Faith* (London: Zed Books).

Robbins, Richard H. (2005) "The History of Technology: The Western Tradition," in Sal Restivo, ed. *The Oxford Encyclopedia of Science and Technology* (Oxford: Oxford University Press).

—— (2009) "Introduction: Globalization and the Environment: A Primer," in Gary Kroll and Richard H. Robbins, eds. *Worlds in Motion: The Globalization and Environment Reader* (Washington: AltaMira Press).

—— (2013) "Coffee, Fair Trade, and the Commodification of Morality," *Reviews in Anthropology*, Vol. 42, No. 4: 243–263.

—— (2014) *Global Problems and the Culture of Capitalism* (Sixth Edition) (Upper Saddle River: Pearson Publishing).

Roberts, Ian (2010) *The Energy Glut: The Politics of Fatness in an Overheating World* (London: Zed Press).

Roberts, Sam (2011) "As the Data Show, There's a Reason the Protesters Chose New York," *York Times*, October 26, A23. 119. http://www.nytimes .com/2011/10/26/nyregion/as-data-show-theres-a-reason-the-wall-street -protesters-chose-new-york.html

Robins, Nick (2006) *The Corporation that Changed the World: How the East India Company Shaped the Modern Multinational* (London: Pluto Press).

Rockström, Johan, et al. (2009) "A Safe Operating Space for Humanity," *Nature* Vol. 461: 472–475.

Rodney, Walter (1972) *How Europe Underdeveloped Africa* (Washington: Howard University Press).

Rosenberg, Justin (1994) *The Empire of Civil Society: A Critique of the Realist Theory of International Relations* (London: Verso).

Ross, Andrew (2014) "Nine Arguments for Debt Refusal," *Strike Debt*, February 7. http://strikedebt.org/nine-arguments/

Rothbard, Murray N. (2002) *A History of Money and Banking in the United States: The Colonial Era to World War II* (Auburn: Ludwig von Mises Institute).

Rowbotham, Michael (1998) *The Grip of Death: A Study of Modern Money, Debt Slavery and Destructive Economics* (Charlbury: Jon Carpenter Publishing).

Roy, William G. (1997) *Socializing Capital: The Rise of the Industrial Corporation in America* (Princeton: Princeton University Press).

Rushton, Steve (2014) "Putting Life before Debt: The Rise of Citizen Debt Audits," *Nation of Change*, 13. http://www.nationofchange.org/putting-life -debt-global-rise-citizen-debt-audits-1397399881

Sadan, Elisheva (1997) *Empowerment and Community Planning: Theory and Practice of People-Focused Social Solutions*. Tel Aviv: Hakibbutz Hameuchad Publishers [in Hebrew].

Samuelson, Paul A. (1964) *Economics: An Introductory Analysis*, 6th Edition (New York: McGraw-Hill).

Sassatelli, Roberta (2007) *Consumer Culture: History, Theory and Politics* (London: Sage Publications).

Sassen, Saskia (2002) "Women's Burden Counter-geographies of Globalization and the Feminization of Survival," *Nordic Journal of International Law*, Vol. 71: 255–274.

—— (2014a) *Expulsions: Brutality and Complexity in the Global Economy* (Cambridge MA: Harvard University Press/Belknap).

—— (2014b) "A Short History of Vultures: Long before Argentina's Latest Default, There Was Elliott Associates," *Foreign Policy*. http://foreignpolicy. com/2014/08/03/a-short-history-of-vultures (accessed April 17, 2015).

Scheper-Hughes, Nancy (2000) "The Global Traffic in Human Organs," *Current Anthropology*, Vol. 41, No. 2: 191–224.

Schild, Verónica (2000) "Neo-liberalism's New Gendered Market Citizens: The 'Civilizing' Dimension of Social Programmes in Chile," *Citizenship Studies*, Vol. 3, No. I. 2: 275–305.

Scitovsky, Tibor (1976) *The Joyless Economy: The Psychology of Human Satisfaction* (Oxford: Oxford University Press).

Scott, W. R. (1912) *The Constitution and Finance of English, Scottish and Irish Joint-stock Companies to 1720* (Cambridge: Cambridge University Press).

Shah, Anup (2012) "World Military Spending." http://www.globalissues.org/ article/75/world-military-spending (accessed April 17, 2015).

Shaw, Martin (2011) "Britain and Genocide: Historical and Contemporary Parameters of National Responsibility," *Review of International Studies*, Vol. 37: 2417–2438.

Sheard, Paul (2013) "Repeat after Me: Banks Cannot and Do Not Lend Out Reserves," *Standard and Poor's Rating Service*, 1–15.

Shilliam, Robbie (2004) "Hegemony and the Unfashionable Problematic of Primitive Accumulation," *Millennium: Journal of International Studies*, Vol. 32, No. 1: 59–88.

Shin, Susan and Claudia Wilner (2013) "The Debt Collection Racket in New York: How the Industry Violates Due Process and Perpetuates Economic Inequality," *New Economy Project*. http://www.neweconomynyc. org/wp-content/uploads/2014/08/DebtCollectionRacketUpdated.pdf (accessed April 17, 2015).

Sieferle, Rolf Peter (2010) *The Subterranean Forrest: Energy Systems and the Industrial Revolution* (Cambridge: The White Horse Press).

Silaen, Parulian and Ciorstan Smark (2007) "Quantification and the Governable Person in Indonesia, 1830–1870," *Journal of Global Business Issues*, Vol. 1, No. 1: 25–33.

Silver-Greenberg, Jessica (2015) "Debt Buyer Faces Fine and Loss of Thousands of Court Judgments," *New York Times*, January 8. http:// dealbook.nytimes.com/2015/01/08/debt-buyer-faces-fine-and-loss-of -thousands-of-court-judgments/?hp&action=click&pgtype=Homepage& module=first-column-region&region=top-news&WT.nav=top-news&_r=1

Sinclair, Timothy (2005) *The New Masters of Capital: American Bond Rating Agencies and the Politics of Creditworthiness* (Ithaca: Cornell University Press).

Skidelsky, Robert (2009) *Keynes: The Return of the Master* (New York: Public Affairs).

Smil, Vaclav (1994) *Energy in World History* (Boulder: Westview Press).

Smith, Jonathan (1948) "The Depression of 1785 and Daniel Shays' Rebellion," *The William and Mary Quarterly*, Vol. 5, No. 1: 77–94.

Soederberg, Susanne (2012) "The Mexican Debtfare State: Micro-Lending, Dispossession, and the Surplus Population," *Globalizations*, Vol. 9, No. 4: 561–575.

—— (2013a) "The Politics of Debt and Development in the New Millennium: An introduction," *Third World Quarterly*, Vol. 34: No. 4, 535–546.

—— (2013b) "The US Debtfare State and the Credit Card Industry: Forging Spaces of Dispossession," *Antipode: Radical Journal of Geography*, Vol. 45, No. 2: 493–512.

—— (2014) *Debtfare States and the Poverty Industry: Money, Discipline and the Surplus Population* (London: Routledge).

Sosin, Jack M. (1964) "Imperial Regulation of Colonial Paper Money, 1764–1773," *Pennsylvania Magazine of History and Biography*, Vol. 88, No. 2: 174–198.

South Park (2009) *Margaritiaville*. Comedy Central. http://southpark.cc.com/full-episodes/s13e03-margaritaville (accessed April 17, 2015).

Speth, James Gustave (2008) *The Bridge at the End of the World: Capitalism, the Environment and Crossing from Crisis to Sustainability* (New Haven: Yale University Press).

—— (2012) *America the Possible: Manifesto for a New Economy* (New Haven: Yale University Press).

Spiro, David E. (1999) *The Hidden Hand of American Hegemony: Petrodollar Recycling and International Markets* (Cornell: Cornell University Press).

Standing, Guy (2011) *The Precariat: The New Dangerous Class* (London: Bloomsbury Academic).

Stavrianos, L. S. (1981) *Global Rift: The Third World Comes of Age* (New York: William Morrow and Company).

Steffen, W., et al. (2004) *Global Change and the Earth System: A Planet under Pressure* (New York: Springer).

Stevis, Matina (2013) "Euro-Zone Bailouts Leave Creditors at a Loss," *Wall Street Journal*, May 30. http://www.wsj.com/articles/SB1000142412788732 44126045785152134158130112

Stiglitz, Joseph (2012) *The Price of Inequality: How Today's Divided Society Endangers Our Future* (New York: W. W. Norton).

Stuart, Hunter (2014) "Debt Collectors Have Figured Out a Way to Seize Your Wages and Savings," *Huffington Post*, June 2. http://www.huffingtonpost .com/2014/06/02/debt-collectors-wages-savings_n_5364062.html

Stuart, J. (1913) *History of the Zulu Rebellion 1906* (London: Macmillan).

Sylla, Richard E. (1998) "U.S. Securities Markets and the Banking System," *Federal Reserve Bank of St. Louis Review*, May–June: 83–104.

Szatmary, David P. (1980) *Shays' Rebellion: The Making of an Agrarian Insurrection* (Amherst, MA: University of Massachusetts Press).

Taylor, Marcus (2012) "The Antinomies of 'Financial Inclusion': Debt, Distress and the Workings of Indian Microfinance," *Journal of Agrarian Change*, Vol. 12, No. 4: 601–610.

Tcherneva, Pavlina R. (2014) "Reorienting Fiscal Policy: A Bottom-up Approach," *Journal of Post-Keynesian Economics*, Vol. 37: 43–66.

Territo, Leonard and Rande Matteson (2011) *International Trafficking of Human Organs: A Multidisciplinary Perspective* (Boca Raton: CRC Press).

Teschke, Benno (2009) *The Myth of 1648: Class, Geopolitics and the Making of Modern International Relations* (London: Verso).

Tett, Gillian (2009) *Fool's Gold: How the Bold Dream of a Small Tribe at J.P. Morgan Was Corrupted by Wall Street Greed and Unleashed a Catastrophe* (New York: Free Press).

Tilly, Charles (1990) *Coercion, Capital and European States, AD 990–1990* (Cambridge, MA: Basil Blackwell).

Tise, Larry E. (1998) *The American Counterrevolution: A Retreat from Liberty, 1783–1800* (Mechanicsburg: Stackpole Books).

Trainer, Ted (2007) *Renewable Energy Cannot Sustain a Consumer Society* (New York: Springer).

Tschoegl, Adrian E. (2001) "Maria Theresa's Thaler: A Case of International Money," *Eastern Economic Journal*, Vol. 27, No. 4: 445–464.

Tucker, Catherine M. (2011) *Coffee Culture: Local Experiences, Global Connections* (New York: Routledge Publishers).

Ubah, C. N. (1980) "Demonetization of Traditional African Currencies under Colonial Rule: The Case of the Manila in Southeastern Nigeria," *Bulletin de l'Institut Fondamental d'Afrique Noire*, Vol. 42, No. 3: 487–501.

Uche, Bhibuike Ugochukwu (1999) "Foreign Banks, Africans and Credit in Colonial Nigeria, c. 1890–1912," *The Economic History Review*, Vol. 52, No. 4: 669–691.

UNCTAD (2007) *The Concept of Odious Debt in Public International Law*. Discussion Paper, No. 185. http://unctad.org/en/Docs/osgdp20074_en.pdf (accessed April 17, 2015).

UNDP (2000) *World Energy Assessment: Energy and the Challenge of Sustainability* (New York: United Nations).

Usher, Alex (2005) *Global Debt Patterns: An International Comparison of Student Loan Burdens and Repayment Conditions* (Toronto, ON: Educational Policy Institute).

Victor, Peter A. (2008) *Managing without Growth: Slower by Design, Not Disaster* (Northamton, MA: Edward Elgar).

Vitali Stefania, James B. Glattfelder and Stefano Battiston (2011) "The Network of Global Corporate Control," *PLoS ONE*, Vol. 6, No. 10: 1–36.

Waldmeir, Patti and Simon Rabinovitch (February 28, 2014) "China Falls Out of Love With Cash," *Financial Times*. http://www.ft.com/intl/cms/s/0/e1469cf0-9cf5-11e3-9360-00144feab7de.html#slide0

Walker, C. E. (1931) "The History of the Joint Stock Company," *The Accounting Review*, Vol. 6, No. 2: 97–105.

Wallerstein, Immanuel (2011) *The Modern World-System*. Four volume history (Berkeley: University of California Press).

Weatherford, Jack (1997) *The History of Money* (New York: Crown Publishers).

Wennerlind, Carl (2004) "The Death Penalty as Monetary Policy: The Practice and Punishment of Monetary Crime, 1690–1830," *History of Political Economy*, Vol. 36, No. 1: 131–161.

—— (2011) *The Casualties of Credit: The English Financial Revolution, 1620–1720* (Cambridge, MA: Harvard University Press).

Williams, Brett (2005) *Debt for Sale: A Social History of the Credit Trap* (Philadelphia: University of Pennsylvania Press).

Williams, Eric (1944) *Capitalism and Slavery* (Chapel Hill: University of California Press).

Williams, William Appleman (1966) *The Contours of American History* (Chicago: Quadrangle Books).

Williamson, Jeffrey G. (2002) "Land, Labor and Globalization in the Third World, 1870–1914," *Journal of Economic History*, Vol. 62, No. 1: 55–85.

Williamson, John (1990) "What Washington Means by Policy Reform," in John Williamson (ed.) *Latin American Adjustment: How Much Has Happened?* (Washington: Institute for International Economics): 5–20.

Winters, Jeffrey A. (1996) *Power in Motion: Capital Mobility and the Indonesian State* (Ithaca: Cornell University Press).

Wolf, Eric R. (1982) (2010) *Europe and the People without History* (Berkeley: University of California Press).

Wolff, Edward N. (2012) *The Asset Price Meltdown and the Wealth of the Middle Class* (Cambridge, MA: National Bureau of Economic Research). NBER Working Paper No. 18559. http://www.nber.org/papers/w18559 (accessed April 17, 2015).

—— (2013) "The Asset Price Meltdown and the Wealth of the Middle Class," *Journal of Economic Issues*, Vol. 47: 333–342.

Wood, Ellen Meiksins (2002) *The Origin of Capitalism: A Longer View* (London: Verso).

Wood, Gordon S. (1969) *The Creation of the American Republic: 1776–1787* (Chapel Hill: The University of North Carolina Press).

Woodward, George W. O. (1966) *The Dissolution of the Monasteries* (London: Blandford).

World Bank (2012) *Global Development Finance: External Debt of Developing Countries* (Washington, DC: World Bank).

World Commission on Environment and Development (1987) *Our Common Future* (Oxford: Oxford University Press).

Wray, L. Randall (1998) *Understanding Money: The Key to Full Employment and Price Stability* (Cheltenham: Edward Elgar).

—— (2002) "State Money," *International Journal of Political Economy*, Vol. 32, No. 3: 23–40.

—— (ed.) (2004) *Credit and State Theories of Money* (Cheltenham: Edward Elgar).

Wright, Robert E. (2008) *One Nation under Debt* (New York: McGraw Hill).

Wrigley, E. A. (2010) *Energy and the English Industrial Revolution* (Cambridge: Cambridge University Press).

Yergin, Daniel (1992) *The Prize: The Epic Quest for Oil, Money and Power* (New York: Free Press).

Young, Brigitte, Isabella Bakker and Diane Elson (eds) (2011) *Questioning Financial Governance from a Feminist Perspective* (London: Routledge).

Young, Stephen (2010) "The 'Moral Hazards' of Microfinance: The Restructuring of Rural Credit in India," *Antipode*, Vol. 42, No. 1: 201–223.

Zehner, Ozzie (2012) *Green Illusions: The Dirty Secrets of Clean Energy and the Future of Environmentalism* (Lincoln, NE: University of Nebraska Press).

Zepezauer, Mark and Arthur Naiman (1996) *Take the Rich off Welfare* (Berkeley: Odonian Press).

Index

Note: Locators followed by "n" indicate the note numbers.